Praise for *One Jewish State*

One Jewish State argues with compelling reason and great passion that keeping God's will to grant Israeli sovereignty over Judea and Samaria offers the best outcome for all the inhabitants of the land—Jewish, Muslim, Christian, and Druze. Whether in terms of security, prosperity, education, or regional cooperation, Ambassador Friedman makes the case that Israeli sovereignty achieves the best result. No one should be surprised that God's vision is, indeed, the best path to peace and prosperity!

> —Mike Pompeo, 70th United States Secretary of State and *New York Times* bestselling author of *Never Give an Inch*

It takes little insight to understand the fallacy of a "two-state solution" to the Israeli-Palestinian conflict, especially after the barbaric assault by Hamas against innocent Israelis on October 7, 2023. But it takes real vision and understanding to offer an alternative. In *One Jewish State*, Ambassador David Friedman brilliantly argues for Israeli sovereignty over all of Judea and Samaria as the best outcome for Jews, Christians, and Palestinians alike and as the means by which to actualize God's will as expressed in the Bible. Ambassador Friedman is uniquely qualified to offer this perspective, and his new book is essential reading for those who seek a better future for the Middle East.

> —Mark Levin, nationally syndicated TV and radio talk show host, chairman of Landmark Legal Foundation, and *New York Times* bestselling author of *American Marxism*

David Friedman is the single most important American-Jewish voice on Israel since Louis Brandeis. His vision is clear, compelling, and realistic. He is not one for useless theorizing or starry-eyed myth-making. Which is why his vision is not only likely to become reality—it may be the only vision that can become reality.

—Ben Shapiro, nationally syndicated radio talk show host, founder of *The Daily Wire*, and *New York Times* bestselling author of *The Right Side of History*

As someone who has been visiting Israel since the summer of 1973, I have long thought that the politicians and diplomats who trumpeted a "two-state solution" were delusional in advocating an impractical, unworkable, and irrational plan that would not result in gains for Arabs who call themselves Palestinians but would only endanger Jews living in their homeland. Repeated rejections and ensuing violence by the Palestinian Authority and every group associated with them should have rendered this long advocated "solution" as outdated and useless as the rotary dial phone, but sometimes bad ideas are just easier than better ones. Ambassador David Friedman dares to deliver a bold idea that serves neither politicians nor diplomats but does serve common sense. I salute him for his creativity and courage, but more importantly for the sound reasoning behind it. This IS the solution the world has been missing.

—Mike Huckabee, nationally syndicated TV talk show host and *New York Times* bestselling author of *The Three Cs That Made America Great*

When history judges those who have globally defended and strengthened Israel, Ambassador David Friedman will be at the forefront. In *One Jewish State*, Ambassador Friedman offers a compelling vision for the future of Israel, grounded in his deep understanding of the Jewish state's biblical history, politics, and enduring challenges. His eloquent and insightful narrative not only explores the complexities of the Israeli-Palestinian conflict but also presents a bold and innovative blueprint for peace and unity for all peoples in the region. Friedman's extensive experience as a diplomat and his unwavering commitment to the Torah and the Promised Land of Israel lend this book a unique and authoritative perspective. A must-read for anyone seeking to understand the nuances of Middle Eastern geopolitics and the path toward a viable and just resolution.

—Pastor John Hagee, nationally syndicated televangelist, founder of Hagee Ministries, senior pastor of Cornerstone Church, national chairman of Christians United for Israel, and *New York Times* bestselling author of *In Defense of Israel*

There is little agreement about the best—or even "least worst"—solution to the never-ending conflict between Israel and Palestinians. One point everyone must agree with is that we need new ideas that reflect the new realities, including October 7. David Friedman is a man of ideas. His ideas, as U.S. ambassador to Israel, helped bring about the recognition of Jerusalem as Israel's eternal capital, the annexation of the Golan Heights, and the Abraham Accords. Now he proposes his most controversial idea regarding Greater or Biblical Israel with significant rights and domestic independence for Arab residents of Judea and Samaria. Whether one accepts or rejects his proposal either as a permanent or temporary solution, it must be considered, studied, and evaluated against other proposals—none of which have gained traction.

—Alan Dershowitz, former Harvard Law professor; noted academic, lawyer, and civil libertarian; and *New York Times* bestselling author of *War against the Jews*

David Friedman was one of the most respected and effective diplomats in the world under President Trump. He strengthened ties between the United States and its most loyal ally, Israel, and helped to negotiate the historic Abraham Accords. In *One Jewish State*, David Friedman shatters the fiction of a two-state solution (rendered all but moot by the Hamas attack of October 7), challenges the anti-Israel bias of the international community, and demonstrates that the best path to peace and prosperity for both the Jewish people and the Middle East is to recognize the reality of Israeli sovereignty over its own land, including Judea and Samaria. Even for those who don't agree, this is a must-read book by one of the most knowledgeable experts and among the keenest observers of Israel and the Middle East in the world today.

—Ralph Reed, founder and chairman of the Faith & Freedom Coalition, CEO of Century Strategies, LLC, and bestselling author of *For God and Country*

ONE JEWISH STATE

ONE
JEWISH
STATE

The Last, Best Hope to Resolve
the Israeli-Palestinian Conflict

DAVID FRIEDMAN

FORMER UNITED STATES
AMBASSADOR TO ISRAEL

Humanix Books
www.humanixbooks.com

This book is written in honor of the soldiers of the Israel Defense Forces, the first responders, and all those who serve in the related security agencies, who rose to defend their nation in its time of dire need. Your courage, commitment, self-sacrifice, and loyalty have saved the Jewish state and inspired the Jewish people. You are owed an enormous debt of gratitude that can never be repaid.

To those lost in battle, or wounded, murdered, tortured, abused, or kidnapped by barbaric terrorists, and to your beloved families, your unspeakable pain haunts all of us. We are with you always. We never will forget you nor will we ever let you down.

This book is dedicated to my parents, Rabbi Morris and Adelaide Friedman, of blessed memory, who instilled in me a fierce patriotism for America and an intense love of Israel, and to Julius and Roslyn Sand, of blessed memory, who instilled the same values in their daughter, Tammy, now my beloved wife of forty-three years.

The Protector of Israel
neither slumbers nor sleeps.

PSALM 121:4

Contents

ONE
JEWISH
STATE

Foreword

I first met Ambassador David Friedman in 2017 when I visited Israel as part of my mission as director of the Central Intelligence Agency. Sitting in the embassy, then in Tel Aviv, I was struck by the ambitious agenda that David had set out for himself. This was no ordinary diplomat focused on bilateral trade and endless social events. Rather, he had real focus and a concrete plan to enhance the United States–Israel relationship in unprecedented ways.

I was not surprised when one of the first people who sought a meeting with me after I had become secretary of state was Ambassador Friedman. He flew from Israel to Washington DC just to make an in-person request that the State Department revisit its policy of many decades regarding the legality of West Bank settlements.

Ambassador Friedman methodically explained to me why the 1978 memorandum of Herbert Hansell, then the chief lawyer at the State Department, was wrong in its conclusion that Jewish settlement in the West Bank was per se a violation of international law. He further argued that this issue involved some real exigency, as the president was working on a "Vision for Peace" involving Israel and the Palestinians that necessitated a shared view of the legal issues involved.

I was sufficiently persuaded by Ambassador Fried-man's presentation to authorize my team to do a deep dive into the relevant issues. Many weeks of work were devoted to getting this right. Ultimately, we concluded that Ambassador Friedman indeed was correct in his arguments, and I issued a directive reversing the Hansell Memorandum and finding that Jewish settlement in the West Bank was not per se illegal. That order became known as the Pompeo Doctrine.

Contrary to the mainstream pundits who saw the Pompeo Doctrine as a dangerous reversal of established precedent, the doctrine recast the Israeli-Palestinian conflict in its proper terms—a dispute for which Israel had a legitimate and compelling legal position. It became a building block within a process that led to the Abraham Accords, the first peace agreements between Israel and Muslim countries in a generation.

After we left office, I had a second opportunity to work closely with Ambassador Friedman. I accepted his invitation to co-star with him in a feature-length documentary film called *Route 60: The Biblical Highway*. *Route 60* takes its audience down the winding road from Nazareth to Beer Sheba, stopping in such biblically significant sites as Shilo, Bethel, Jerusalem, Bethlehem, and Hebron. *Route 60* premiered at the Museum of the Bible in Washington, DC. It then screened in 1,100 theaters in September 2023, where it enjoyed immense popularity.

I was always impressed by David Friedman's political and diplomatic insights as an ambassador. As a filmmaker, however, I was struck by his deep knowledge and love of the land that he and now I refer to as Judea and Samaria. His ability to connect biblical history and text to the sites that we visited, and to draw lessons from each of those sites, was remarkable.

I am delighted that Ambassador Friedman has written a new book called *One Jewish State*, in which he draws upon his knowledge and experience to propose a new way of thinking about the Israeli-Palestinian conflict. He eschews the conventional diplomacy directed toward a two-state solution, which has failed and brought misery to the inhabitants of the region for decades. Instead, he takes us in a different direction.

Ambassador Friedman begins with the words of God and the prophets, so beautifully expressed in the Old Testament, in which the land of Israel is promised to the Jewish people. He then argues, with compelling reason and great passion, that keeping God's will to grant Israeli sovereignty over Judea and Samaria offers the best outcome for all the inhabitants of the land—Jewish, Muslim, Christian, and Druze. Whether in terms of security, prosperity, education, or regional cooperation, Ambassador Friedman makes the case that Israeli sovereignty achieves the best result. No one should be surprised that God's vision is, indeed, the best path to peace and prosperity!

As Israel continues to suffer through its most difficult year since its founding, it desperately needs new and creative thinking, from within its own society and from its allies, to emerge secure and confident and to recover from its trauma. And it needs to reconnect with its majestic biblical legacy that has seen it through so many challenges in the past. Israel is the only ancient society still in existence precisely because it has clung to its holy books.

One Jewish State, by Ambassador David Friedman, presents exactly that type of thinking. It may not be the only solution to the Israeli-Palestinian conflict, but its recommendations should be on the table and up for discussion whenever and wherever the issue arises.

Michael R. Pompeo
The 70th United States Secretary of State

Author's Note

Please Read This with an Open Mind

This book challenges the most widely accepted but fatally flawed concept in Middle Eastern diplomacy: the two-state solution. It is an odd name for a policy that is anything but a "solution." Indeed, for more than fifty years, U.S. and world leaders—some with good intentions, some without—have tried without success to implement this policy. The efforts have brought nothing but failure and misery.

A two-state solution, if implemented, would force Israel to take territory that it captured fair and square from Jordan when Jordan made the fateful decision in June 1967 to attack Israel and give that land to Palestinians who have never before had a country, have no track record of running a country, have no popular mandate because of endemic corruption within their society, and in far too many cases, just want to kill Jews and destroy Israel. No wonder it's gone nowhere.

The two-state solution is more than a bad idea, however. It is a formula for a never-ending conflict. Diplomats in the United States, the United Nations, the European Union, and elsewhere throw billions of dollars toward the Palestinians to virtue signal their support, to buy protection so as not to be terrorized themselves, and to raise expectations of a Palestinian state even though everyone knows they won't materialize. Every few years, the money runs out because it has been pocketed by corrupt leaders or invested in terror assets, the expectations that were never realistic are dashed, and another war begins in which Palestinian terrorists attack Israeli civilians. Israel, of course, responds—carefully and surgically, seeking to minimize civilian casualties—and then the world reflexively sympathizes with the Palestinian aggressors because they are the weaker party. This results in more money being sent to the Palestinians, more corruption, more anger, and another war. It is an endless cycle of violence, and it never improves because the world refuses to recognize the obvious: the Palestinians should not have, and many of them have told me they don't even want, their own state!

Adding a massive insult to the already massive injury of Palestinian terrorism, the land that the world wants Israel to surrender to the terrorists is Judea and Samaria, referred to by most as the West Bank. This is the heart of Biblical Israel, where the ancient kings of Israel ruled and the prophets preached. Surrender of this territory would put some of the holiest sites on earth for Jews and Christians into the hands of people who want nothing more than to eradicate the biblical sanctity of this land. To millions of Christians and Jews, this surrender is also decidedly against God's will.

The Jewish people are called Jews because they come from Judea, part of the kingdom ruled over by King David and King Solomon. The notion of Judea not being part of the Jewish state of Israel, as demanded by the Palestinians and nearly all of the world, is untenable and part of a larger goal to decouple the Jewish people from their biblical homeland.

As an observant Jew, and particularly since the Hamas massacre of October 7, 2023, I feel as if God is calling out to us and admonishing, "How many more times do I need to convince you not to surrender the land that I have given to you for eternity?"

I hope October 7 was the last time.

But this book is not just about ending the two-state solution. It's also about replacing it with a structure that works for all. While some will presume that this book is hostile to the Palestinians because it rejects Palestinian statehood, it is hostile only to their failed leadership and to those committed to hatred and violence. To those willing to consider a more hopeful and peaceful region, this book presents a realistic plan to bring the Palestinians out from under their own largely self-induced misery: a plan that follows the lessons of the Bible and applies them to the complex facts on the ground, to thread the needle in a manner that is true to the dignity of every human life and to the biblical covenants of God.

The State of Israel has not known a single day of peace in its seventy-six-year history. It remains in a state of war with Lebanon, Syria, and Iraq and with terrorist groups such as Hamas, Hezbollah, and Islamic Jihad. Although Israel is a party to peace treaties with its other neighbors Jordan and Egypt, that peace is exceptionally cold and often strained. Most of Israel's diplomatic challenges, however, are not with these local players. Its greatest challenges have come from the United States, the EU, the UN, and others who presume to know better than Israel what is best for Israel.

It's time to let Israel be Israel, to support its democratically elected leaders to fulfill the will of its citizens. Israel wants peace far more than any of the chattering elites with Ivy League degrees who have never served a day in battle or known the anguish of losing a child in the defense of a nation. Given enough runway to plot its own course, I believe that Israel will embark on a realistic path to peace. I think that plan will look a lot like the contours presented in this book.

Each chapter of this book tackles an issue relevant to resolving the Israeli-Palestinian conflict. Like the trial lawyer that I used to be, I will present different blocks of evidence that may not immediately appear connected to the ultimate point. But stay with this until the closing argument, and it should all come together.

Please read this with an open mind. My hope is that this book becomes a topic of serious discussion and perhaps even the handbook for the last and best chance for Middle East peace.

David Friedman
June 2024

1
THREE SIMPLE WORDS

I call this book *One Jewish State* for the movement that I have begun to lead—a movement to create a safe, secure, and prosperous State of Israel within its biblical homeland in a manner that brings security, human dignity, prosperity, and pride to each and every one of its inhabitants.

Each of these three simple words is deeply infused with meaning beyond what may appear at first glance.

For starters, let's consider the implications of the word *one*. There is only one Jewish state: the State of Israel. There are more than thirty Muslim countries and many Christian, Buddhist, and Hindu countries but only one Jewish state, taking up a land mass about the same size as New Jersey. The world bristles at the idea of a *single state* dedicated to the Jewish faith and the Jewish people on the land in which Jews have resided for more than three thousand years. No other nation faces that challenge. Israel is the *one and only* nation, among 193 members of the United Nations, that is a Jewish state. There must always be room in this world for one Jewish state.

There is, of course, additional meaning to the word *one*, now more important than ever. Not only is there only one Jewish State, *but there can never be more than one Jewish state.* History tells us—from as far back as the days of Solomon to as near in time as the judicial reform protests in Israel just last year—that the Jewish people are extremely vulnerable when they are divided. One Jewish state means a united State of Israel. Once united around the principles enumerated in this book, there is nothing that Israel cannot achieve.

* * *

Now let's turn to the second word, Jewish. The Jewish state of Israel is exactly that—JEWISH. It is the place where Jewish history was born, where Jewish values were created, and where more Jews live than anywhere else in the world. It is situated on the land given to the Jewish people by God in the words of the Holy Bible.

What are some of the places that make the State of Israel Jewish?

Well, let's start with Jerusalem, Israel's eternal capital. A capital established by King David some three thousand years ago to unite the Jewish nation. The Dome of the Rock—the gold dome that adorns almost every landscape photo of Jerusalem's Old City—sits on the Temple Mount purchased by King David as the site of the holy temple, as recounted in the books of Samuel and Kings. Two magnificent temples stood there, one after the other (each ultimately being destroyed by foreign enemies), for almost one thousand years in total, many centuries before that dome was built. Going back even further, the rock that sits inside that gold dome is said to be the stone upon which Abraham passed God's test of faith and received God's covenant to this holy land.

The Temple Mount in Jerusalem looks across a valley to the Mount of Olives, site of the oldest Jewish cemetery in the world (some three thousand years old) and across a second valley to Mount Zion. The word Zion is another name for Jerusalem, and Zionism is the political movement, begun in the nineteenth century, to restore the Jewish nation to their biblical homeland with Jerusalem as its capital. The last verse of Israel's national anthem, "Hatikvah," speaks of the modern State of Israel being a free nation in its homeland in the land of Zion, Jerusalem.

Another ancient biblical site is Hebron, from which King David ruled during the first seven years of his reign. This is where Abraham purchased a burial cave for his wife Sarah. Ultimately, it became the burial place as well for Abraham, Isaac, Jacob, Rebecca, and Leah—all but one (Rachel) of the Jewish patriarchs and matriarchs. That biblical cave remains today a place of deep prayer and spiritual connection.

Here's another one—Bethel. This city is mentioned more times in the Bible than any other city except Jerusalem. It also is a town in almost every state in the United States. This is where Jacob had his famous dream of a ladder reaching up to the heavens with angels ascending and descending. It is where God promised Jacob that he would honor the pledge he made to his grandfather Abraham and father, Isaac, and give this land to the Jewish people forever. It is the place to which Jacob was returning when he wrestled with an angel and had his name changed to "Israel" because he had wrestled with God and man and had prevailed.

In May of 2022, I filmed *Route 60: The Biblical Highway*, a documentary about Judea and Samaria that I co-produced with Matt Crouch of the Trinity Broadcast

Network (TBN), which co-starred Secretary of State Mike Pompeo along with me. We traveled Route 60—a winding road along which so much of the biblical narrative occurred. In addition to Jerusalem, Hebron, and Bethel, we filmed Shilo, Bethlehem, Rachel's Tomb, Mount Gerizim, Mount Ebal, Joseph's Tomb, and of course, the Old City of Jerusalem.

Every single one of those places spoke to me. Each holy site enabled me to immerse myself in biblical history and to walk the steps of the biblical heroes and heroines that so inspire hundreds of millions of people.

The lessons of two particular locations, off the beaten path, remain with me now, especially during this period of trauma for the Jewish people: Rachel's Tomb and Joshua's Altar.

Rachel was one of Jacob's two wives, along with her sister Leah. She was the mother of Joseph and Benjamin. Rachel died while giving birth to Benjamin. Recounting her burial, Genesis 35:19–20, says, "And Rachel died. She was buried on the road to Efrat—now Bethlehem. Over her grave Jacob set up a pillar, it is the pillar of Rachel's grave to this day."

Rachel did not die that far from Hebron, the burial place of Abraham and his progeny. Yet Jacob sought to bury her in a nondescript location, a place that even today is very modest in its size and appearance. And yet Rachel's Tomb receives many visitors every day, especially from people who are suffering.

There was always something very special about Rachel. She suffered for a greater cause, beginning when she deferred marrying her beloved Jacob for seven years so that her older sister, Leah, could marry first. She represents the quintessential characters of the Jewish people—perseverance and a willingness to endure suffering with the faith of ultimately prevailing.

Jeremiah the prophet, who lived about one thousand years after Rachel, offered God's words of comfort to Rachel in Jeremiah 31:15–16—words that inspired the creation of the State of Israel:

> This is what the Lord says:
>
> A voice is heard up high
> Mourning and great weeping
> Rachel weeping for her children
> And refusing to be comforted
> Because they are no more.
>
> This is what the Lord says:
>
> Restrain your voice from weeping
> And your eyes from tears
> For your work will be rewarded
> Declares the Lord
> They will return from the land of the enemy
>
> So there is hope for your descendants
> Declares the Lord
> Your children will return to their own land.

Today, Israel suffers in the manner of its matriarch Rachel. It cries for her children because they are no more. But Israel also lives with hope and confidence, just as God said in comforting Rachel, that her children will return to their own land.

Another moving but little traveled place in Judea and Samaria is Joshua's Altar, located on the downslope of Mount Ebal. Notwithstanding its significance, it is almost impossible to find, with no signage whatsoever.

As he approached the end of his life, Moses, the greatest prophet in the Bible who spoke directly with God, knew that no matter how much he pleaded, God would not let him lead the Jewish nation across the Jordan River into the land of Israel. Stoically, Moses offered this directive from God to Joshua, his successor, in Deuteronomy 27:5–6:

> So when you've crossed the Jordan, erect these stones on Mount Ebal. Then coat them with plaster. Build an altar of stones for God, your God, there on the mountain. Don't use an iron tool on the stones.

When Joshua brought the Israelite nation across the Jordan River, building the altar was not his initial task. First, he had the Jewish men circumcised; then he conquered Jericho; then he had a mishap with the Kingdom of Ai, losing his first battle with great trauma but winning the second time; and then he built the altar.

The book of Joshua 8:30–31, recounts:

> Then Joshua built on Mount Ebal an altar to the Lord, the God of Israel. As Moses the servant of the Lord had commanded the Israelites, he built it according to what is written in the Book of the Law of Moses—an altar of uncut stones, on which no iron stone had been used.

This episode is such a powerful lesson in leadership. Joshua takes over for Moses and begins the process of leading the Jewish nation. He begins as a general—a fighter—but not fully a leader. It is only when he understands where he stands within the continuum of Jewish life—as a successor to Moses, who left him with specific instructions, and a servant of God responsible to actualize

God's ancient biblical covenants—that Joshua becomes a true leader. He became that leader with the construction of that altar on Mount Ebal in accordance with Moses's direction and God's specifications. As I explain later in this book, the Jewish people fully became a nation—Am Yisrael—when Joshua built that altar.

To visit that altar, especially if you have had the fortune of serving your country, is to visit a place of enormous inspiration. It leads to an important understanding of the role of faith, the essential value of humility, and the need to maintain one's mission.

But perhaps the most important takeaway of this history lesson is the following: All these places that I have described, places of massive religious consequence and historical majesty, are not part of Israel under the views of virtually every nation. Even Israel itself, while it maintains control over these sites, has been reticent to provoke international condemnation by declaring its sovereignty over any of these places outside of Jerusalem. I would challenge even an experienced traveler to comfortably visit more than a few of these locations. It's not easy.

But these holy places, and so many more within the land of Israel, are living proof of the glorious heritage of the Jewish people. They provide the quintessential Jewish DNA that connects Jews across continents and across generations. This land and the biblical covenants and wisdom emerging from within it are what makes Jews Jewish.

Israel is referred to by many as the "Land of the Bible." Were that really true! So much of Biblical Israel is mired in decades-old disputes that place Israel's God-given sovereignty in doubt. These disputes also fuel a reservoir of resentment, stagnation, and violence that prevents advancement within the region. It's time to break this logjam, and with the clarity brought about by the October 7 massacre, the real solution—indeed, the only solution—is now evident.

* * *

And finally, the last of our three words, "state," is no less important. Israel is not just a territory. It is not an amorphous location like "Palestine," a name given by the Romans to Judea to signify their conquest of ancient Israel. Indeed, to commemorate the Jews' defeat, Rome minted a coin saying "Judea Capta"—Judea has been captured.

Palestine was never a country and never governed itself. Israel is very different. As a state, it has both the responsibility and the opportunity to lead its residents to a better place: a place of peace, dignity, and prosperity; a place where God's covenants to Abraham, Isaac, and Jacob can finally be actualized.

The State of Israel is a sovereign nation. But Israel's sovereignty over portions of its biblical homeland is challenged by many around the world and even some within Israel itself. Israel, however, can never fully be a Jewish state without sovereignty over the territory that makes it Jewish. As a sovereign state, Israel, and only Israel, can bring closure to this critical issue. I believe it should do so in the manner discussed within this book—a manner that incorporates God's will as expressed within the Bible. And at this special time in history, God's instructions and commandments also clearly present the best outcome for all of Israel's inhabitants. If we all just took a step back and did an overlay of biblical wisdom on geopolitical realities, the convergence that we would perceive would be striking. It would lead many around the world to support Israel in this effort.

The barbaric massacre committed by Hamas against innocent Israelis on October 7 was the worst attack against the Jewish people since the Holocaust and has brought great trauma upon the State of Israel. The fact that more than 80 percent of Palestinians in Judea and Samaria have endorsed that attack only deepens the pain. But the assault also has brought great clarity, albeit at a staggering human cost. It is this clarity that tells us we need a fundamentally new approach. It is this clarity that tells us Israel must plan its future on its own and not obsess about what others think. And it is this clarity that compels us to go back to basics—to return to the biblical values and divine covenants that unite the Jewish people and provide a clear path forward.

The State of Israel was founded by people of great courage and vision, and they rose to the challenge of building their state in defiance of overwhelming odds. But the challenges only grew with time. There was never the luxury of convening something akin to a constitutional convention for discussion and reflection in order to address the big-picture items on the agenda: the terms of a national constitution, a comprehensive plan for the role of religion within the state, the best means by which to integrate minorities into society such that their loyalty to the Jewish state was secure, and the appropriate national borders. Each of these issues was handled with surprising skill given that everything was done under fire. But it was done piecemeal and hardly compared with the type of intellectual rigor that preceded the adoption of the United States' foundational documents.

When the war with Hamas ends and the threat from Hezbollah abates, Israel will have massive issues to resolve—big budgetary constraints, rebuilding challenges, addressing the physical and psychological trauma of so many wounded and killed, and so much more. But it also needs to make the effort—as a sovereign state—to take a step back and tackle this big issue: How does Israel best remain and enhance its status as both the one Jewish state and a state that bestows dignity, kindness, and prosperity upon all its inhabitants in a manner befitting a Jewish state? This book attempts to help that process along.

The agenda of "One Jewish State" sounds simple and noncontroversial. It is anything but. Nonetheless, it is the only long-term path to a just and peaceful resolution to the conflicts that have plagued this region for centuries. The details, historical context, and supporting arguments appear in the chapters that follow.

2

UNFINISHED BUSINESS

We were sitting around the Oval Office on June 23, 2020, about to discuss Israel's planned assertion of sovereignty over approximately 30 percent of Judea and Samaria, or as some people call it, the "West Bank." It had been almost six months since President Trump and Prime Minister Netanyahu stood together on January 28, 2020, in the East Room of the White House and jointly announced a plan upon which Israel would negotiate peace with the Palestinians. A key feature of the plan would permit Israel to assert this sovereignty right away, even in the absence of Palestinian support. And the United States would support that move and recognize Israel's expanded borders.

But things quickly went off the rails on the sovereignty recognition, as key players from both sides (myself included) had different understandings and perspectives on how this process would unfold. On June 23, 2020, we finally set down to iron those out once and for all.

It was a crowded room, but there were really only three protagonists: Secretary of State Mike Pompeo and me, speaking in favor of sovereignty, and President Trump, who wanted to understand why this issue required his attention at a time when the United States was almost completely shut down by the COVID-19 pandemic.

Before even publishing our plan, I wanted to make sure that the State Department was fully on board with the notion that Israelis had the legal right to live within Judea and Samaria. Most of the world felt, and continues to feel, differently, and I was unwilling to put out a plan that might then be declared illegal by our own government. During 2019, I worked extensively with lawyers from the State Department and Israel's Ministry of Foreign Affairs to get this right. We reached the conclusion—we'll get into this more a bit later—that international law *did not* prohibit Jewish settlement in Judea and Samaria, and Mike Pompeo so declared that to be the position of the United States on November 19, 2019. His statement became known as the "Pompeo Doctrine."

As we gathered that day in the Oval Office, President Trump was not particularly concerned with the efficacy of the Pompeo Doctrine. He had more basic questions: How would this partial assertion of sovereignty lead to a more peaceful region? What would happen to the other 70 percent of the territory? Would it become even more radicalized?

Mike and I went back and forth on this with the president. Mike focused on the fact that we had made a commitment to Israel on sovereignty, and we should keep our promises. I argued that the Palestinians needed to see that the train was leaving the station—that this plan would proceed with or without them—and a partial recognition of sovereignty would send that signal clearly and prompt more realistic negotiations.

It was obvious from his demeanor that President Trump did not consider this to be his most pressing issue.

After more back and forth, he told Secretary Pompeo that he trusted him and that he should do the right thing. We took that as an unenthusiastic endorsement of sovereignty but an approval nonetheless.

As the days passed after that meeting, an avalanche of world leaders and domestic politicians weighed in with the president in opposition to sovereignty. I had returned to the embassy in Jerusalem, where Jared Kushner called to tell me that while President Trump had not officially changed his mind, he was moving in that direction.

I was contemplating another visit to the Oval Office when our path suddenly took a different course: We got a message from the United Arab Emirates that it would consider full normalization of relations with Israel if Israel would shelve its sovereignty plans. It was a stunning opportunity—peace with a prominent Gulf nation without any concessions of territory and not subject to a Palestinian veto. Negotiations ensued and were successful, culminating in what became known as the Abraham Accords.

On the issue of sovereignty, I negotiated on behalf of the United States and Israel. We agreed only to the "suspension" of a sovereignty declaration for four years. I made it clear that while we had Israel's commitment to negotiate with the Palestinians based on our plan for those four years (even though Mahmoud Abbas, the chairman of the Palestinian Authority, already had bashed the plan in a public tantrum at the United Nations), once the four years were up, there would be no restrictions on a sovereignty declaration by Israel.

So here we are today, and the four-year suspension of sovereignty has expired. Where do we go from here?

I confess that I was elated on that late summer day, September 15, 2020, when the Abraham Accords were signed on the South Lawn of the White House. But for me, there was a bittersweet component in deferring what would have been an equally historic and positive development in Israel's brief history: the recognition of Israel's sovereignty over parts of its biblical homeland. Since that date, we have only drifted farther from that goal.

Since that meeting in the Oval Office, I have thought about how Israel and the United States should manage this unfinished business regarding Judea and Samaria. I have spoken at numerous settings in Israel and challenged the audience to draw a map of its borders. They can't. Some think Israel's eastern border—its longest border—is the Jordan River, and others say it's the "Green Line"—the armistice line of 1949 drawn to create a cease-fire boundary, but not an agreed upon border, after the 1948 War of Independence. Still others point to the "Allon Line" drawn by General Yigal Allon or refer to the boundaries of the "settlement blocs" without a clear definition of what is within those "blocs."

My point to my Israeli friends is that this issue must be decided by Israel for Israel. There is no shortage of interest around this issue by the United States, the European Union, Russia, and the United Nations. I promised my audience that if this issue is decided, God forbid, by any of these players, no one in Israel will be happy with the outcome.

My message to Israel is that it must begin a national conversation regarding the future of Judea and Samaria, reach a consensus determination as to where Israeli sovereignty must reach, and then make the case to the world why this is a good and fair plan. As I say at the end of every speech, the world will respect Israel when Israel respects itself.

While not the only consideration for this decision, Israel cannot ignore its biblical legacy. It's a subject that draws a bit of discomfort within many segments of the Israeli population, undoubtedly because God's presence is so powerfully enmeshed within the fabric of the land of Israel, many fear that to acknowledge it is to be overwhelmed by it. But this need not be the case. Indeed, I think it's the right time to embrace God's will.

I've had lots of discussions with Israelis of all backgrounds and beliefs about Judea and Samaria. The following conversation is fairly typical and may surprise you.

Over the past few years, I have met with many Israeli hi-tech entrepreneurs to explore the possibility of investing in their companies. The conversation usually begins with some general introductions, then extends to the particular business or technology under consideration, and always ends with a discussion of Israeli and U.S. politics.

During one such discussion, I learned that the Israeli businessman in front of me—a highly successful engineer—was a lifelong resident of Tel Aviv, intensely patriotic, and devoutly secular. His comments prompted me to ask him if he believed in God and he responded that, as a child of Holocaust survivors, he had difficulty accepting that a God existed who could have permitted such atrocities to occur. I understood.

I asked him, "What do you think about Judea and Samaria, the West Bank?"

His response did not surprise me. "To tell you the truth, I don't want it. I haven't been there since the army, and I have no interest in my children risking their lives so that we can rule over Palestinians against their will."

I followed up by asking him if he understood the connection of this land to the Jewish people. I said to him, "For example, do you know what happened in Shilo?" He did not know but gave me the opportunity to explain.

"After the great exodus from Egypt, Moses brought the Jewish nation north along the eastern side of the Jordan River where they encamped from place to place until they got to the mountains of Moab where Moses died. Joshua then takes over and brings the nation across the Jordan River into what is now Samaria and, after a few stops, encamps in Shilo. The ark of the covenant and the mobile tabernacle rested in Shilo, which became the capital of the Jewish nation for some 369 years. It is the first place where the Jews stopped wandering—it was their first home."

To my surprise, he was at rapt attention, either because the subject was so interesting or because of his shock that a former U.S. ambassador knew so much about the Bible. Or both. I continued, "Shilo was where Joshua assigned territory to the Israelite tribes. It is also where Hannah taught the world how to pray."

"What do you mean, 'She taught the world how to pray?'" he jumped in.

"Well Hannah desperately wanted a child. And so, she went to the tabernacle and began to whisper a prayer to God. No one had ever done that before. It was so unusual that Eli, the high priest, thought she was drunk. But she was just speaking with God from her heart and God answered her with a son—Samuel the prophet."

I then got to the bottom line. "So my friend, here is the choice. There is Shilo and twenty more places just as biblically significant as Shilo in Judea and Samaria. You are Israeli, this is your decision: to keep it and fight for it, if necessary, or to give it away to people that will likely destroy these sites and prohibit Jews from ever going there. What should Israel do?"

His response was immediate and unequivocal. "We have to keep these places! This is who we are, this is our DNA. Whether we believe, or don't believe, or have doubts, these places have sustained the Jewish people for 3000 years. It's the reason we are here, and all the other ancient peoples are in museums."

I've heard that response again and again, even from Israelis who considered themselves entirely secular! Once they gain an understanding of the biblical majesty of Judea and Samaria instead of just reading about the daily friction and international condemnation associated with these sites, their perspectives often change.

The modern State of Israel, for all its inspiration and beauty, still has not achieved sovereignty over much of the territory within which our Judeo-Christian heritage is embedded—the land upon which God commanded Abraham, Isaac, and Jacob to lift up their eyes and envision as the divine Jewish homeland. And we need to find a way to correct this.

As I write this book and attempt to delineate the path forward, I think back to the comments made by President Trump on that memorable day in the Oval Office: "How will sovereignty lead to a more peaceful region?"

Some Americans and Israelis have pushed for sovereignty over Biblical Israel since Judea and Samaria was captured from Jordan in 1967, with the Israeli movement taking the lead. But so far no one has given much thought to, let alone answered, President Trump's overriding question: How will sovereignty make the region more peaceful and prosperous?

The Israeli right, which includes some incredible patriots, has never been able to articulate a full vision for the region. Most have advocated for sovereignty over the Jewish settlements located in what is referred to as "Area C" since the disastrous Oslo Accords. None have offered a solution for Areas A and B—the territory that Oslo placed under almost complete Palestinian control. But carving out Area C for Israel while leaving Areas A and B to fend for themselves would ultimately turn those areas into Gaza—isolated hotbeds of angry Palestinians who undoubtedly would grow their existing terror network.

Imagine replicating Gaza right in the center of Israel. The challenges faced by Israel now from hotbeds of terrorism in places like Jenin, Nablus, and Ramallah would expand until millions of Israelis are in the line of fire. It doesn't have to be that way. While today Israel must contend with a hostile Palestinian population that overwhelmingly supports the attacks of October 7, in regaining control over all of Judea and Samaria, Israel can begin a process of better policing and neutralizing the terrorists while rewarding and incentivizing Palestinians who wish to participate in a project that will greatly improve their lives. It's a "carrot and stick" approach instead of just a stick.

Trump was looking for a win-win, not a win-lose or a lose-lose. And since that meeting in the Oval Office on June 23, 2020, I have thought about how it can be achieved. That's the unfinished business that this book hopes to begin finishing.

3
THE CONVERGENCE OF FAITH AND POLICY

Faith and policy normally don't mix. Faith is something hard to prove; it is a conviction regarding the existence of God, his engagement in the momentary events of the world and every human life within it, and the revelation that God's will is reflected in the holy texts and the words of the prophets.

A person of real faith will attempt to live his or her life in accordance with God's commandments. Those commandments are the subject of debate and interpretation, but they all find their home in the Old Testament for Jews and Christians, with the New Testament providing additional divine authority for those of the Christian faith. The Bible still matters. By some accounts, it still sells more than two thousand copies *every hour*!

In the United States, no one is supposed to make public policy based on faith. Indeed, a common criticism of half-baked proposed policies that are poorly defended is "faith is not a policy." Instead, one pushing a public policy agenda needs data, data, and more data. In making foreign policy decisions in particular, we tend to analyze multiple factors to determine our national interest. Those considering how we might structure our relationship with Israel often evaluate data concerning what the United States derives commercially, militarily, and politically from that relationship; how the relationship affects our national security; and what costs we might bear and what opportunities we might lose in connection with our relationships with Israel's enemies if we side with Israel.

The final decision regarding U.S. foreign policy is, of course, made by the president. I was present in the room when President Trump listened to his foreign policy team and made decisions regarding Israel—in his case the most favorable decisions for Israel of any president in history—and I have read with interest the writings of those who recounted that deliberative process that they observed with other presidents. In seemingly all cases, decisions were made based on a balancing of issues including national security, politics, and the economy. But not faith. Faith may have influenced the hearts and minds of those present, but no one ever raised faith as a significant factor.

One Middle Eastern policy that has lived, breathed, and flourished within the bowels of the massive Harry S. Truman State Department Building in Washington DC is the centrality of a "two-state solution" for Israel and the Palestinians. It is the "mother's milk" of our foreign policy, embraced, at least until now, by many Democrats and Republicans alike. This so-called solution is not only claimed as a means to bring peace, prosperity, and democracy to Israel and the Palestinians, but it is ensured to quiet the entire Middle East and stabilize the region.

The "two-state solution" took form with the Oslo Accords of 1994. It didn't matter that Palestinian terrorism increased 400 percent in the year following Oslo, with buses full of Israeli women and children literally being blown up on a steady basis, along with suicide bombers wreaking havoc in hotels, restaurants, and other public places. The "peacemakers" plowed forward then and every year since, ignoring the undeniable evidence that Palestinians don't want a state alongside Israel; they want a state instead of Israel.

Many people of faith, however, cannot support a two-state solution. While understanding the enormous security risks that such a scheme imposes upon the State of Israel, that's not their primary objection. Instead, many in the Christian community, especially Evangelicals, and some in the Jewish community, especially the Orthodox, oppose the two-state solution as a matter of their religious beliefs.

People of faith recognize that the land of Israel was given to the Jewish people by God. And if God gave this land to the Jews, no one has the right to undo that grant.

Indeed, in the book of Genesis, God makes a separate covenant with each of the three Jewish patriarchs—Abraham, Isaac, and Jacob—that this land will be given to them and their progeny:

To Abraham, God promised, "Because all this land that you see I have given to you and your progeny forever" (Genesis 13:15).
To Isaac, God promised, "For to you and your descendants I will give all these lands and will confirm the oath I swore to your father Abraham" (Genesis 26:3).

> And to Jacob, God promised, "I am your God, the God of your father Abraham and Isaac, the land upon which you are resting I will give to you and your progeny" (Genesis 28:13).

These covenants have inspired Jews to live in their biblical homeland, often at great personal risk. Jews have lived in the land of Israel continuously since the days of Joshua.

The land given to the Jews is central to their faith. In the Jewish religion, observance of God's commandments is said to lead to the Jewish people flourishing within the land. Conversely, abandoning those commandments can lead to expulsion from the very same territory. Jews who live outside of Israel are considered to be in "exile"— indeed, the full actualization of the Jewish faith simply cannot be accomplished outside of Israel.

During the long history of the Jewish presence within the land of Israel, however, it has been the rare exception that Jews have ruled over the entirety of their nation from a capital in Jerusalem. Such periods, few and far between, were during the reigns of King David and King Solomon (seventy-three years during the tenth century BCE), parts of the Hasmonean Dynasty (in the first and second centuries BCE), and of course, the government of modern Israel from 1948 to the present.

Modern Israel established Jewish rule over the land of Israel for the first time in more than two thousand years, and understandably, those of us lucky to be alive during this period see the Hand of God at work. When, in 1967, Israel defeated its enemies in just six days of war, reunified Jerusalem, and regained control of Judea and

Samaria, many people of faith saw the actualization of God's will.

Many in the Muslim world appreciate Israel wanting to retain its holy sites. I once spoke with a high-ranking sheikh from a Gulf country and asked him how Israel could, in good conscience, surrender places imbued with such holiness in the Old and New Testaments. He was sympathetic. He acknowledged that no Muslim country would surrender its holy places and that he supported Saudi Arabia in not permitting non-Muslims from entering Mecca and Medina, Islam's two holiest places. But he observed that Jews and Christians have not fought for their biblical heritage as fiercely as Muslims. He wasn't wrong.

I've often marveled at the respect given by the West to the Islamic faith. Liberal feminist journalists like Christiane Amanpour are only too happy to cover their entire bodies and most of their faces with a hijab when interviewing Muslim leaders. They show respect because respect is demanded of them. Jews and Christians unfortunately are less insistent that their faith be respected. That's a mistake.

I won't forget an "off the record" speech I made to the Conference of Presidents of Major Jewish Organizations in Jerusalem in 2018. The conference is an umbrella organization that includes the leaders of fifty of the leading Jewish organizations in the United States. I was asked what I thought of the two-state solution, and I answered that I thought it was impossible. I noted that in such a construct, the Palestinians required that their "state" be devoid of Jews (or "Judenrein" as the Nazis used to say). I added that there was no way that a half million Jews living in Judea and Samaria would ever abandon their faith and voluntarily leave their homes to make room for a Palestinian state, it was unlikely that the Israeli army would ever force such an evacuation, and that if such a decision were made, it likely would lead to a civil war within Israel.

The left-wing representatives at the conference immediately leaked my comments to the press (in violation of the ground rules) with much outrage that I was acting against a two-state solution. They were delusional. In 2005, Israel, under Prime Minister Ariel Sharon, withdrew all its citizens—nine thousand Jews—along with its entire military presence from the Gaza Strip in a move that now looks absurdly foolish. That evacuation of just nine thousand Israelis from a remote portion of Israel almost caused a civil war. And the consequences of that evacuation—a terror state on Israel's border—proved to be disastrous. Given that reality, I was undoubtedly correct that hundreds of thousands of Jews living in Israel's biblical heartland in Judea and Samaria would never leave and no Israeli government would force them. And yet the liberal wing of American Jewry was stunned that someone would tell them that their political agenda was just a fantasy, and a bad one at that.

Politics and faith have thus collided over Israel, at least since 1967. Most politicians of both U.S. parties, along with the United Nations and many world leaders, have pushed for Israel to transfer Judea and Samaria to the Palestinians to establish a state of their own. So prevalent was this view that anyone opposed to a two-state solution, notwithstanding the violence brought about by the Oslo Accords, was deemed "anti-peace." In contrast, members of the faith community advocated that "not one inch" of God's territorial grant to the Jewish people could be given away, least of all to enemies of the State of Israel with blood on their hands.

For most of the history of this conflict over Judea and Samaria, the politicians had the upper hand. They controlled the policies of their respective countries, and none were prepared to endorse Jewish settlement of Israel's biblical homeland. But failure to endorse was not tantamount to an ability to stop Israeli expansion. As the political class droned on and on about the need for a Palestinian state in Judea and Samaria, Palestinian terrorists continued to poison any appetite among Israelis to reward them with territory, and Jews increasingly settled in the land promised to their ancestors. Today there are almost one million Jewish Israelis living in East Jerusalem and Judea and Samaria.

Prior to October 7, 2023, internal debate within the U.S. government had been one-sided about the future of Israel's biblical homeland. In the State Department, few—if any, other than Mike Pompeo and I—pushed for Jewish settlement. Most American Jewish organizations were neutral to negative on Jewish settlement as well. But everything changed on that catastrophic day.

October 7 saw 1,200 innocent people, mostly Jewish civilians, murdered and another 254 taken hostage by Hamas. While every murder is an abomination and an affront to God's laws, these killings were particularly barbaric. Women were sexually abused and raped, children were forced to watch the murder of their parents, and parents witnessed the execution of their children. Babies were burned and beheaded. And much of this carnage was captured on film by Hamas terrorists themselves. Unlike even the Nazis who were reluctant to reveal the full extent of their crimes, Hamas joyfully and triumphantly recorded the most brutal of its assaults. Simply put, October 7 was the worst day for the Jewish world since the Holocaust.

October 7 and its aftermath demonstrated that the Palestinian dispute with Israel is not territorial, and it is not political. It is not about borders, and it is not about conflicting opinions on international law. Rather, this dispute is about the right of the Jewish people to exist at all and to live within their biblical homeland.

This isn't a news flash. Anyone paying attention since the early twentieth century knows that Israel's Arab neighbors wanted no Jews living between the Jordan River and the Mediterranean Sea. Those chanting today "From the river to the sea Palestine will be free" are indeed just echoing a century-old position.

By the blood and toil of its founding pioneers and every generation since, Israel has won and maintained its freedom and independence. Egypt and Jordan have simply given up on the fantasy of trying to destroy Israel. But Syria and Lebanon—in partnership with Iran—have not. And most Palestinians harbor unbridled hatred for Israelis, many of whom, to their credit, have resisted the urge to hate them back in return.

Reliable polls taken after the October 7 massacre revealed that some 85 percent of Palestinians living within Judea and Samaria support what Hamas did on that dark day. The murder of Jewish women and children, the rape of young girls, and the burning of babies is considered by most Palestinians as not just an acceptable but even a commendable method of vindicating their grievances against Israel.

Exactly what grievances were "vindicated" by the October 7 massacre no one could say. With Israel's evacuation from Gaza in 2005, not a single Jew remained in the territory, and not a single military officer operated there. Israel left behind hotels and farms and greenhouses that had produced much of Israel's produce.

Within a year of Israel's departure, the people of Gaza elected Hamas as their leaders. But that did not bring a halt to financial assistance from around the world. The United Nations, the Palestinian Authority, the Gulf States, and even the USA infused massive "humanitarian" aid into the Gaza Strip. But instead of using those funds to assist its population, Hamas used most of the money to build rockets and terror tunnels.

Well before Israel even reacted with its defensive operation in response to October 7, many on the far left, especially within elite U.S. and European academic institutions, expressed their support for what Hamas did, in some cases voicing their "exhilaration" regarding the attacks. But it became even worse.

The Biden administration, initially supportive of Israel's right and obligation to "eradicate" Hamas, began to notice that its position was wildly unpopular among the progressive left on college campuses as well as the cities with large concentrations of Arab residents like Dearborn, in the swing state of Michigan. While Israel was fighting for its life, Biden began his fight for reelection. Taking his lead and advancing politics over principle, traditionally pro-Israel Democrats like Chuck Schumer and Nancy Pelosi began to turn on Israel. They pushed for an end to the fighting even while more than 120 hostages remained in captivity. In a nutshell, they pushed for a Hamas victory.

These Democrats then doubled down on a plan that was both tone-deaf and clearly overtaken by events—a two-state solution. And with this, they unintentionally put the nail in the coffin on this dangerous and outdated plan.

Supporters of Israel on the center and the right, and virtually everyone in the Republican Party, now see the two-state solution not as a fair outcome but as a "final solution" (Hitler's famous phrase advocating genocide) for the Jewish state. Seeing the hatred in the hearts of Palestinians, their capacity to inflict unspeakable harm and then to celebrate those acts of cruelty, left any reasonable person with the certitude that Israel cannot cede territory to these people who will just use that land as a platform from which to kill more Jews. Fantasies of "kumbaya moments" between Israelis and Palestinians gave way to the harsh reality that the only "solution" relevant to Israel was its survival.

Arabs have murdered Jews in the Holy Land for centuries, with the Hebron Massacre of 1929 beginning the murderous opposition to a modern Jewish state. Sadly, of the handful of innovations attributed to Palestinian society, the most noteworthy is the suicide bomber—the troubled youth fitted with a wardrobe of explosives and promised an eternity with seventy-two virgins if he blows himself up along with a crowd of Israelis.

I learned of this psychotic tactic firsthand the evening before my cousin was to be married in Jerusalem in 2003. That evening, the bride met her father at a café to catch up after the dad had returned from a business trip in the United States. A suicide bomber trained by Hamas detonated himself inside the café, and the bride and her father both perished. My cousin, the groom, threw what was to be his wedding ring into her grave in anguish.

But with the magnitude of the October 7 assault and its unprecedented cruelty, the disqualification of the Palestinians as peace partners is now complete. Notice I said the "Palestinians" and not just "Hamas." While many Palestinians support Hamas, as we will discuss, the Palestinian Authority—representing the so-called good Palestinian leadership—is just as hateful and perhaps even more corrupt.

There's also the matter of economics. A Palestinian state, apart from being a terror threat, would continue the economic failures of the Palestinian Authority. The GDP per capita of the Palestinian Authority is an abysmal $2,500. Other Arab nations in the vicinity are not much better—Jordan, Egypt, and Lebanon are at about $4,000, and Syria is under $1,000. There is no question that a Palestinian state will fare no better than any of its Arab neighbors, none of which are democracies.

A Palestinian state, if ever created (God forbid), is likely to fail economically in the same manner as its neighbors. This, in turn, will accelerate the radicalization of the Palestinian people and increase the already strong likelihood that "Palestine" will become a terror state.

In contrast to its Arab neighbors, Israel's GDP per capita is about fifty-four thousand dollars, placing it within the world's top twenty nations. That's more than twenty times the production of the Palestinian Authority.

This goes a long way to explaining why the two million Arabs who are citizens of Israel live peacefully inside a Jewish state. The opportunities for Arabs—Christian and Muslim—in Israel are unrivaled anywhere in the Middle East. In Israel there are world-class universities attended in droves by Arab men and women. Arabs in Israel have risen to the pinnacle of industry, medicine, science, technology, and academia.

In the aftermath of October 7, as students around the world ignorantly shouted for Palestine to replace the State of Israel, by and large Israeli Arabs did not join that refrain. Why would an Israeli Arab want to see his or her economic opportunity reduced by 95 percent? Why would an Israeli Arab want to live in a corrupt autocracy and surrender his or her freedoms?

For Palestinians to prosper, to live free and to achieve the human dignity that they deserve, the only demonstrable pathway is inside Israel. That doesn't mean this can be achieved overnight, and there still remains the challenging imperative to weed out terrorists from within the Palestinian population. But the future for Palestinians only shines brightly if it is within the Jewish state.

When I came to Israel as the U.S. ambassador in May 2017, my initial role was limited to the bilateral relationship between the United States and Israel. Two months later, I was named to the "peace team" to explore the possibility of peace between Israel and various Arab parties. Then in early 2019, the Jerusalem Consulate—the de facto embassy to the Palestinians—was closed and merged into the embassy, giving me an area of responsibility that included Gaza and the West Bank.

As a result, I was privileged to spend a good amount of time with Palestinian leaders and ordinary people. What I took away from these meetings was that the leadership pressed for Palestinian statehood primarily for the purpose of ensuring a steady flow of funds from wealthy nations coerced into sponsoring that project. At the same time, the ordinary people had absolutely no confidence that their lives would be any better—most felt they would be worse—under a Palestinian state.

I saw that Palestinians would be receptive to life under Israeli sovereignty if accompanied by the opportunity for better health, education, and prosperity and the assurance of human dignity.

Since October 7, faith, politics, security, and economics all converge in assessing the Israeli-Palestinian conflict. Now more than ever before, they all lead to the same place—to the expansion of Israeli sovereignty over its biblical homeland in Judea and Samaria and to the gradual integration of Palestinian Arabs into the Israeli economy. This will keep Israelis and Palestinians safe, secure, and eventually prosperous.

Should any of us be surprised that God's plan for the land of Israel is also the best path forward for all the land's inhabitants? If anything, we should be surprised at how long it has taken to appreciate this obvious reality. Nonetheless, with the clarity brought by the tragic massacre of October 7, the truth stares us right in the face.

We'll now spend some more time understanding the intellectual, social, legal, and theological underpinnings of Israeli sovereignty over Judea and Samaria.

4

A RELIGION AND A NATION

There are many forms of antisemitism, but perhaps the most dangerous, because it is the most prevalent, is the claim that one can embrace the Jewish religion while still condemning the presence of Jews in their own state in the land of Israel. It can't be done, even as there are many who attempt to draw this distinction.

Much of the secular world struggles with the notion of a Jewish nation. Like Christianity and Islam, they see Judaism as a religion. One can be a perfectly good Christian or Muslim living anywhere in the world. Why isn't the same true of Judaism?

Judaism is indeed different. Its theology is inextricably tied to the land of Israel. God's covenants to the Jewish patriarchs, discussed earlier, all relate to Jewish sovereignty over that land. As we will soon discuss, the prophecies of Isaiah, Jeremiah, and Ezekiel—and even Moses—speak to the expulsion from, and then the return of the Jews to, their land. And the prayer books of every stream of Judaism all beseech God to restore the Jewish people to Zion and Jerusalem.

The point is perhaps best made by the author of Psalm 137 (some say King David, others suggest a different author who actually experienced the Babylonian captivity), who writes from the "rivers of Babylon" in verse 4, "How can we sing God's songs on foreign land?" The author thus states in the most fundamental of terms that the faith of Israel and the land of Israel cannot be separated.

Since the destruction of the Second Temple in Jerusalem in the year 70 CE, Jews around the world prayed—literally every single day—that their eyes should see God's return to Zion. They add, in their prayers, "To Jerusalem, your city, may you [God] return with mercy, and may you dwell within it as you have spoken, and build it permanently soon within our days, and may you prepare the seat of King David within that city, blessed are you our Lord, the builder of Jerusalem."

The duality of faith and nationhood for the Jewish people is as old as the Bible itself.

It begins, of course, with faith: with Abraham, who heard God's voice and left his home in Haran, in what is now Turkey, and traveled to the city of Shechem in the Promised Land. Although he was the first to find faith in a single God, and although God promised that he would make the progeny of Abraham into a great nation, that nation was not yet named or in existence. Indeed, only one of Abraham's two sons, Isaac (and not Ishmael), would enter the line of succession of the Jewish people. Abraham wasn't even called a Jew but rather an "Ivri"—a Hebrew and literally one on the other side of the masses.

Abraham's son Isaac confronted the same issue as his father. Of his twin sons, Jacob and Esau, only the former was deemed worthy by God to carry on the building of the nation of Israel.

And then came Jacob. With his two wives and two concubines—Leah, Rachel, Bilhah, and Zilpah, respectively—he fathered twelve sons. Jacob's name then became Israel, and each of his twelve sons became the leader of a tribe. The twelve tribes were then referred to in the Bible collectively as the "Children of Israel."

But the Children of Israel were not yet a nation. They lived, oddly enough, in Egypt under the protection of their brother, uncle, and great-uncle Joseph, who had risen to be second only to the ruling Pharaoh. But when Pharaoh died, a new monarch emerged who did not know Joseph. And he enslaved the Children of Israel.

It was while in Egyptian slavery that the Children of Israel were forged together as a people with a collective identity. But they still were not yet referred to as a nation.

Moses, of course, brought the Children of Israel out of Egypt and across the divided Red Sea. He brought them to Mount Sinai, where they heard the word of God proclaim the Ten Commandments. Through Moses they were taught the remainder of the Torah—the laws and values around which they were instructed to guide their lives.

But the Children of Israel, having found faith and having shared a common national experience in the exodus from Egypt and the revelation at Sinai, are still not referred to in the Bible as the nation of Israel.

That status is only achieved when the Children of Israel enter the land of Israel under the leadership of Joshua. Joshua brings them across the Jordan River at what is now called "Qasr al Yehud"—the "bridge of the Jews" (where John the Baptist is said to have baptized Jesus)—and begins the conquest of the land promised by

God. The Children of Israel proceed to defeat the cities of Jericho and Ai.

But they are still not yet called the nation of Israel. They suffered together in Egypt, they heard God's word at Sinai, and they fought their enemies in battle, but they had not yet sought God's blessings in the land of Israel. That was achieved when Joshua built an altar on the downslope of Mount Ebal and carved his own texts on the local stones, as he was commanded to do while still in the wilderness.

The scene is perfectly described in the book of Joshua 8:33:

> All the Israelites, with their elders, officials and judges, were standing on both sides of the ark of the covenant of the Lord, facing the Levitical priests who carried it. . . . Half the people stood in front of Mount Gerizim and half of them in front of Mount Ebal, as Moses the servant of the Lord had formerly commanded when he gave instructions to bless the *nation of Israel.*

The Bible uses the words "Am Yisrael" here for the first time, the same words we use today as we call out "Am Yisrael Chai"—the nation of Israel lives.

The Jews thus were not deemed a nation without both milestones achieved by Joshua on that historic day: (1) fulfilling a commandment of God (2) within the land of Israel. Together, the spiritual and the territorial achievements fused together to make Israel a nation. No other faith bears this characteristic.

Indeed, there are "mitzvot"—God's commandments to the Jewish people—that only can be performed within the land of Israel. In biblical times, when Israel largely was an agricultural society, there were commandments addressing the tithes that were required to be given from one's crops to the priests, the Levites, and the poor; there were requirements for much of the land to lay fallow during the sabbatical (seventh) year; and there were numerous strictures regarding how and when certain produce could be harvested and consumed. All these commandments applied only to agriculture within the land of Israel.

One of God's commandments unique to the land of Israel that affected me personally was the obligation to give the first wool shorn from a sheep to the priests.

One day toward the end of my term as ambassador, I received a call from a farmer living in the Golan Heights. To this day, I don't know how he got through to me.

The farmer raised sheep and asked me if he could bring the first wool shorn from his sheep to the U.S. embassy in Jerusalem to present to me since I am a Kohen—a descendant of the priestly class of Israel. He was referring to the commandment contained in Deuteronomy 18:3–4:

> This is the share due the priests. . . . You are to give them the first fruits of your grain, new wine and olive oil, *and the first wool from the shearing of your sheep.*

My curiosity got the better of me and I agreed to meet the farmer. He came to the embassy with a wicker basket full of ratty, untreated wool and placed it in my hands while reciting a blessing. I then asked him what I should do with this gift, and he offered to take back the wool, clean it and spin it into four fringes for my Tallit—my prayer shawl. I agreed.

A few weeks later I was presented with a Tallit with the fringes spun from the new wool. I have worn it every day since during my morning prayers. I have received many mementos and awards from my time in service, but this gift ranks at the very top. It reflects the observance of one of God's commandments that can only be performed in the land of Israel.

God's blessings and punishments to the Jewish nation also are tied to the land. In the second stanza of the "Shema," the most significant prayer and biblical text within the Jewish faith, the Jewish nation is reminded that the observance of God's commandments will lead to "rain for your land" and "grass for your fields," such that the inhabitants of Israel may prosper. However, God also warns that the failure to follow his decrees will lead to the nation "perish[ing] quickly from the good land that the Lord is giving you."

The greatest calamities that have befallen the Jewish people over the years have resulted in their exile from the land. The saddest day on the Jewish calendar is the ninth day of Av, when the First Temple in Jerusalem was destroyed by the Babylonians in 586 BCE and the Second Temple was destroyed by the Romans in 70 CE. In both cases, the destruction was followed by lengthy periods of exile for many Jews displaced from their land. We mourn those exiles to this day.

But above all else, the restoration of the Jewish people in the land of Israel is the subject of essential biblical prophecies.

Moses was the first to predict the return of the Jews even though he never experienced their expulsion from their land. Nonetheless, as the greatest prophet in Jewish history, he saw it coming. As the book of Deuteronomy comes to a close, Moses foresees that the nation of Israel will sin against God and be uprooted from the land of Israel. But then he envisions their return to God and resulting resettlement within the Promised Land. He writes, in 30:2–5,

> And you will return to the Lord your God with all your heart and with all your soul, and you will listen to his voice according to all that I am commanding you, this day you and your children. Then the Lord, your God, will bring back your exiles, and he will have mercy upon you. He will once again gather you from all the nations where the Lord, your God, had dispersed you. Even if your exiles are at the end of the heavens, the Lord, your God, will gather you from there and he will take you from there. And the Lord, your God, will bring you to the land which your forefathers possessed, and you will take possession of it, and he will do good to you, and he will make you more numerous than your forefathers.

Moses's words are enormously powerful and emotive, foretelling the ingathering of the Jewish exiles from the most remote corners of the earth. It is not difficult to see how this prophecy, during the two-thousand-year gap with respect to Jewish sovereignty over the land of Israel, became ingrained within the Jewish faith.

And other great Jewish prophets, all of whom actually experienced the fall of the Jewish empire to the Babylonians, saw things the same way.

The prophet Isaiah explains in Isaiah 11:12, "And He shall raise a banner to the nations, and he shall gather the lost of Israel, and the scattered ones of Judah He shall gather from the four corners of the earth."

The prophet Jeremiah speaks of a similar divine redemption after exile. He envisions, in Jeremiah 29:14, "And I will be found by you, says the Lord, and I will return your captivity and gather you from all the nations and from all the places where I have driven you, says the Lord, and I will return you to the place whence I exiled you."

And finally, there is the great prophecy of Ezekiel regarding his vision of the Valley of the Dry Bones. God commands Ezekiel to hear his message over a mass grave of bones, whereupon the bones grow flesh and connective tissue, are restored to life, and march out from within the valley. God then explains to Ezekiel with great dramatic and emotional effect in Ezekiel 7:11–14,

> Then he said to me: Son of man, these bones are the people of Israel. They say "our bones are dried up and our hope is gone; we are cut off." Therefore, prophesy and say to them: "This is what the sovereign Lord says: My people, I am going to open your graves and bring you up from them; I will bring you back to the Land of Israel. . . . I will put my spirit in you and you will live, and I will settle you in your own land."

The restoration of the Jewish nation within the land of Israel is the absolute essence of biblical faith and prophecy. And it has been actualized over the past century with the rebirth of the modern State of Israel. The realization of these biblical prophecies is viewed by many as the most significant theological development of the past two thousand years.

In April of this year, 2024, as anti-Zionist movements across the United States grew in strength and volume, far-left Jewish journalist Naomi Klein wrote an article at the beginning of the Passover holiday entitled "We need an exodus from Zionism." Seeing her post her piece on X, I responded, "You are welcome to exit Judaism, but you can't exit Zionism and remain Jewish. God's covenants to Abraham, Isaac and Jacob and the Prophets all validate the Jewish people living freely in their Biblical homeland. This is immutable and the essence of our faith."

The response from Jewish progressives was quick and merciless. Many pointed to some fringe ultra-Orthodox groups who condemn Zionism. Others expressed disgust that I would take it upon myself to decide who was Jewish and who wasn't.

Of course, I was not deciding anything. I was just reading the Bible and relaying its message. People are free to reject Zionism, and some Jews have. But they are then rejecting one of the core theological principles of the Jewish faith. Could a Christian remain one after denying the sacrifice of Jesus? Could a Muslim reject the Koran? There are fundamental principles that define every faith. Zionism is central to Judaism.

There are ultra-Orthodox Jews who reject Zionism because they see it as a secular movement, and they would like to see Israel run exclusively under Jewish Halachic law (e.g., no public transportation anywhere on the Sabbath; no nonkosher food). Personally, I am against religious coercion, as are many Orthodox Jews—I would prefer to see Israelis embracing Judaism of their own free will, and we see evidence that this is occurring in large numbers. But those ultra-Orthodox are not denying the biblical holiness of the land of Israel—they actually are affirming it with great intensity.

Judaism is thus both a religion and a movement of national independence. It is unlike any other faith in this regard. In recent times, many have come to defend their anti-Zionism by spouting platitudes about other aspects of Judaism they deem worthy. It is fake theology. Jewish settlement in the land of Israel is an inextricable component of the Jewish faith.

Jews pray for their complete return to the land of Israel, Jewish ritual is best performed—and on occasion only performed—within the land of Israel, and the Jewish people did not exist as a nation until they entered the land of Israel. The biblical prophets saw Jewish redemption as only occurring by the restoration of the Jews within the land of Israel.

The land and the faith, the religion and the nation, cannot be disconnected.

5
WHO ARE THE PALESTINIANS?

Few categories of people garner more attention and world sympathy than the Palestinians. Yet they are far from the most disadvantaged on the planet. The Uighurs are held in concentration camps in China; there are African tribes subject to wholesale slaughter; Syrian civilians in the millions died or were displaced in its civil war over the past decade; the Kurds are persecuted and remain stateless, as are Tibetan Buddhists ruled by China, whose leader, the Dalai Lama, lives in exile. Meanwhile, Palestinians already are the majority in Jordan, almost two million of them are full citizens of Israel, and there are millions of Palestinian emigrants living abroad with no desire to return home. One example of many is Mohamed Hadid, by law a Palestinian refugee, who left Nazareth shortly after Israel's independence to build mansions in Bel Air and Beverly Hills. His daughters went on to become pro-Palestinian models from the comfort of Southern California. The United Nations considers all the Hadids to be refugees entitled to assistance.

Who are these people?

The simple answer is that the Palestinians are people who lived in Palestine, but that would include Jews as well. Prior to the establishment of the State of Israel in 1948, there were Palestinian Arabs and Palestinian Jews.

For two thousand years, after the destruction of the Second Temple in 70 CE, Palestinian Jews prayed to be restored as a nation in the land of Israel, as they already had been for the prior millennium. For the first five hundred of those two thousand years, there were no Palestinian Arabs. Arabs arrived in Palestine with the Muslim invasion around the year 600 CE.

Never, prior to the creation of the State of Israel, was there a national movement for an Arab Palestinian nation in this land held sacred by the Jews.

After Israel came into existence as a modern state, the Palestinian Arabs took the name Palestinian exclusively for themselves. The Palestinian nationalist movement was begun by Yasser Arafat in 1964. It was not a movement to create a nation but a terror organization to drive Israel into the sea. In reality, the term Palestinian originated as a brand, not a people. And a violent brand at that.

The term Palestine goes back nearly two thousand years. The territory was formerly known as "Judea," named after Jacob's son Judah and constituting much of the land of Israel, including Jerusalem. After the Second Temple was destroyed by the Romans in the year 70 CE, many Jews escaped to the northern part of the country. About sixty years later, the Jews made one last attempt to reconquer Jerusalem through the revolution inspired by their leader, Bar Kochba. Three years into the war, in 135 CE, the revolution was defeated.

By this point, the Romans wanted to obliterate any signs that Jews once ruled this land. The name Judea—so closely associated with Jewish rule—was eliminated, and the Romans sought a new name that would bring maximum humiliation upon their Jewish enemies. They chose "Syria Palestina" or Palestinian Syria. The name Palestina was derived from the Hebrew word Plishtim, which translates to Philistines—the biblical archenemy of the Jewish nation during the days of the judges, the prophets, and the early kings of Israel. Changing Judea to Palestine was thus the Roman means of putting an exclamation point on Rome's defeat of the Jewish nation.

The only thing that the Roman name change of Judea to Palestine has in common with the appropriation by modern Palestinian Arabs of the name for themselves is that in both cases, the transition was designed to harm the Jewish people. In the case of Rome, it was the final act of its victory. In the case of today's Palestinians, it was the first step in a movement to destroy Israel.

When the name Palestine emerged in 135 CE, there were no Palestinian Arabs to adopt it. As already noted, there was no Arab presence in Palestine for another five hundred years, until the advent of Muslim invasions of the land. Even as the Palestinians appropriated this brand in the mid-twentieth century, they succeeded to a name they could not even pronounce. Palestinians do not have the letter "P" in their lexicon. They pronounce "P" as a "B" and thus decided to refer to their appropriated nationality as "Falastin."

Many books have explored in great detail the emergence of a Palestinian national movement. We won't do that here, but it is necessary to provide some basic historical context for how we have come today to deal with a

Palestinian movement that considers itself, as does much of the world, entitled to statehood.

Not only has there never been a country called Palestine, but for centuries, there weren't even any borders for Palestine—not being a country and not having sovereignty over any particular territory, it wasn't relevant. It was all just a land mass within the Ottoman Empire. That needed to change with the conclusion of World War I as the Ottoman Turks relinquished their claim to Palestine.

The victorious powers in World War I issued mandates for governance of much of the territory that they conquered. The British received the mandate for Palestine and then proceeded, for the first time, to draw the borders for that territory. They negotiated the northern border with the French, who received the mandate for Syria (which included Lebanon), and the southern border with the nascent Kingdom of Saudi Arabia.

Under the British mandate for Palestine, the territory extended to what is today referred to as Gaza, Israel, Judea and Samaria (the West Bank), and Jordan. In 1946, the British transferred the Palestinian territory east of the Jordan River to the newly established Hashemite Kingdom of Jordan. With that, approximately 72 percent of British Mandatory Palestine was no longer subject to administration under the mandate.

The Kingdom of Jordan is thus a Palestinian state—a state created from almost three-quarters of Palestine. To this day, a majority of the inhabitants of Jordan are Palestinians as well. But the kings of Jordan—there have been four since the founding of the kingdom—have strenuously resisted being referred to by this reality. Jordan does not seek to absorb any more Palestinians—they want another Palestinian state to be created elsewhere.

After 1946, the British mandate had shrunk to just Gaza, Israel, and Judea and Samaria. By international law, this territory was earmarked as a homeland for the Jewish people. These rights derived first from the Balfour Declaration of 1917, whereby the British government undertook to favor the establishment of a national home for the Jewish people in Palestine without prejudice to the civil and religious rights of existing non-Jewish communities. The Balfour Declaration was then put into effect pursuant to the San Remo Resolution adopted on April 25, 2020, by the "Principal Allied Powers" of the First World War—Great Britain, France, Italy, and Japan (with the United States participating as an observer). Coupled with Article 22 of the new League of Nations, the San Remo Resolution instructed Britain to act as a trustee for Palestine in accordance with the precepts of the Balfour Declaration until Jewish statehood could be achieved.

The British mandate for Palestine failed. The British were never able to achieve statehood for the Jewish people and oversaw numerous deadly revolts by the Arab population of Palestine. Massacres of Jews by Arabs occurred often under British rule, including in Hebron in 1929 (249 killed), Jaffa in 1936 (over 300 killed there and in close proximity), and Jerusalem in 1948 (55 killed). By 1939, Jewish militias formed and began to fight back, initially against their Arab attackers but then against the British authorities as well.

In 1939, Britain announced that, notwithstanding its mandate to facilitate a national homeland for the Jewish people, it would restrict Jewish immigration into Palestine to a trickle. This devastating announcement coincided with the impending slaughter of Jews throughout Europe by Nazi Germany and the creation of hundreds of thousands of European Jewish refugees, many with no place to go. Jewish paramilitary groups fought the British to gain access to Palestine for Jews escaping from Europe with limited success.

The Balfour Declaration was clear on its face, but the British simply would not bring it to life. They saw enormous commercial opportunities with newly formed oil-rich Arab nations and were not about to ruin those relations for poor Jewish refugees. But with Jews being gassed in Europe, they couldn't just permit an Arab holocaust in Palestine. Instead, they punted the issue to several commissions to address the "Jewish question."

The Peel Commission of 1937 was the most noteworthy. It concluded that Jews and Arabs could not coexist in Palestine. They were just too different, and the Arab malevolence toward the Jews was unlikely to abate. The commission resolved that the territory must be split between Jews and Arabs with the holy places in Jerusalem enjoying neutral status. The Arab countries vehemently rejected this recommendation. Most of the leaders of the Jewish settlement in Palestine were also against this recommendation. They had understood that all of Palestine would be available for Jewish habitation in accordance with the Balfour Declaration. Ultimately, however, David Ben-Gurion and Chaim Weizmann, on behalf of the Jewish settlement, offered conditional approval.

In light of the Arab rejection of the Peel Commission's recommendations, the British appointed a second body—the Woodhead Commission—to delve into the logistics and practicalities of partitioning Palestine. That commission decided that the challenges were too great, and the plan was shelved.

The League of Nations had contemplated that the mandates granted around the world would all lead to sovereign states. By the end of World War II, this had occurred for every mandatory territory other than Palestine. Throughout the world, the mandatory powers had succeeded in cleaning up the mess caused by World War I by creating independent states to engage in self-governance. But not in Palestine—the Arab nations would not agree to live with a Jewish state on any terms and on any borders!

By 1946, the United Nations had succeeded the League of Nations, and the issue of Palestine was assigned to UNSCOP—the United Nations Special Committee on Palestine.

In October of 1947, UNSCOP issued its report and recommendations once again advocating for the partition of Palestine into a Jewish state and an Arab state with a special regime for Jerusalem. On November 29, 1947, the UN, by about a 75 percent majority, endorsed the Partition Plan. The plan was accepted by the Jewish leadership and rejected by all Arab nations. Jewish leaders were disappointed with their allocation of territory—its borders were indefensible. But there were over one million Jewish refugees in European displaced person camps, and statehood was essential to absorb these lost souls.

During this entire period from 1917 through 1948, there was no Palestinian party engaged in the decision-making process regarding the outcome for Palestine. Rather, there were Arab nations bordering Palestine who voiced their rejection—Jordan, Egypt, Syria, Lebanon, Iraq, and others.

The British prepared to leave after the Partition Plan was approved. They had failed to create an independent state within the mandatory territory for which they assumed responsibility. On May 14, 1948, they departed Palestine, leaving the Palestinian Jews and Arabs to fend for themselves.

That same day, Ben-Gurion declared Israel's independence from a library in Tel Aviv as the United Nations had authorized. In short order, five Arab nations attacked Israel, seeking to push the Jews into the Mediterranean Sea. Fortunately, they failed. The war came to a temporary end in 1949 with an armistice agreement that established a line upon which a ceasefire would be maintained. That line is colloquially referred to as the "Green Line." Critically, the Green Line was rejected by all five Arab countries as the border upon which the conflict would be settled. The Arabs reserved the right to push Israel into the sea on another occasion.

From 1949 through 1967, Judea and Samaria, along with the Old City of Jerusalem, were under Jordanian control. Jews had been evicted from Jerusalem in 1948 and were denied access by Jordan to their holy places. During this period, Palestinian nationalism began to develop, not as a means to obtain independent statehood in Judea and Samaria (which was then held by Jordan), but rather as a means to destroy Israel.

Throughout history, there have been many nationalist movements. In many cases, those movements have actually led to a new nation. Where successful, there invariably has been a people bound together by a common history, culture, and value system. Israel certainly would count as a successful nationalist movement on this basis. The United States as well.

Palestinian nationalism, however, lacked any cohesive principles for nationhood apart from a hatred of Israel. There was no common history; no foundational culture, art, or literature; and no national aspirations toward self-governance. Palestinians were Arabs; they were largely Sunni Muslim, and they were tribal. Some were Bedouin and nomadic. Palestinians had almost nothing in common from tribe to tribe that set them apart from the Arab populations of Israel's neighbors.

The Palestinian Liberation Organization (PLO) was founded in May 1964. Its charter sought to acquire for the Palestinian people the entirety of mandatory Palestine and to bring an end to Zionism. What Palestine would look like after the PLO had defeated Zionism was less of an issue. Whether the PLO would create a democracy, a theocracy, or a monarchy was not addressed. Would the post-Zionist regime afford any human rights to its inhabitants? Again, not contemplated. It's no wonder why the PLO failed and today is reviled by the overwhelming majority of Palestinians. The movement never advanced beyond Jew hatred.

In June of 1967, Israel won the Six-Day War, and things were never the same. In that war, Israel reunited Jerusalem and captured the Golan Heights from Syria, Judea and Samaria from Jordan, and Gaza and the Sinai Peninsula from Egypt.

Ultimately, Israel returned Sinai to Egypt pursuant to a peace treaty; it asserted its sovereignty over Jerusalem and the Golan Heights, with United States' approval coming in the Trump administration; it evacuated its citizens and its army from Gaza in 2005; and it continues to control parts of Judea and Samaria.

Although Jordan supports a Palestinian state, at no time during Jordan's nineteen years of control over Judea and Samaria did the Palestinians or any of their leaders ask Jordan to create a state for them in that territory.

It simply wasn't relevant until Israel gained control. Because the Palestinian demand for statehood within Judea and Samaria was always about destroying Israel.

The PLO was led by Yasser Arafat. He had competition in his efforts to lead the Palestine liberation movements. There was the Popular Front for the Liberation of Palestine (PFLP), the Democratic Front for the Liberation of Palestine (DFLP), Black September, and later Hamas, Palestinian Islamic Jihad (PIJ), and the Al Aqsa Martyrs Brigade. None of these groups competed for the hearts and minds of the Palestinians living in Israel or Judea and Samaria. Rather, they competed for who could kill the most Jews in the most brutal manner.

The Palestinians have little for which to be proud of their leaders. Their one invention, if one can call it that, was terrorism. Palestinians hijacked the first airplane in 1968—an El Al flight from Rome to Tel Aviv. It was the only El Al flight ever hijacked.

Four years later, Palestinians committed perhaps the most famous act of terror before September 11, 2001: the Munich Olympic Massacre. In July 1972, an organization called Black September, an affiliate of the PLO that got its name from its attacks against Jordanian officials in September 1971, murdered eleven Israeli athletes and coaches. The terrorists all escaped with little resistance from the West German authorities.

Black September struck again in 1973, at an El Al ticket counter in Athens, Greece. Shooting with submachine guns, they killed three and injured some fifty-five. In 1974, the DFLP took 115 students and teachers hostage in an elementary school in Ma'alot in Northern Israel. Thirty-one were murdered and seventy were injured.

These were just some of the many terror attacks in the 1970s, mostly under the leadership of Arafat. And it continued in the 1980s. On October 7, 1985, four PFLP terrorists hijacked the cruise ship *Achille Laoro* and threw overboard Leon Klinghoffer, a Jewish man bound to a wheelchair. On July 6, 1989, a PIJ terrorist seized a crowded public bus and drove it off a cliff near Jerusalem, killing sixteen and injuring twenty-seven. And there were many more similar attacks.

Terror attacks by Palestinians continued through 1993, arising to a more organized violent revolution referred to as the First Intifada. Instead of concluding with the defeat of its enemy, Israel instead brought the First Intifada to a close with the first of the Oslo Accords: a series of amorphous agreements intended to lead to a Palestinian state in much of Judea and Samaria.

A key component of the Oslo Accords was a commitment by Arafat to nullify the covenant within the PLO charter that Israel must be destroyed. Arafat repeatedly spoke from both sides of his mouth, agreeing at times to withdraw the covenant while telling his base, in Arabic, that the Palestinian armed struggle would never end. Apart from the PLO, no other Palestinian terror group accepted the Oslo Accords, and to this day, the covenant has never formally been rescinded. To be sure, Arafat and his successor have offered lip service and correspondence negating the covenant, but the withdrawal required the approval of the Palestinian Legislative Council, which to date has only "assign[ed] its legal committee with the task of redrafting the Palestinian National Charter" to effectuate the necessary amendments (per the 1996 Amendment to the Palestinian National Charter). We are still waiting to see the "redraft."

President Clinton, whose administration actively brokered the Oslo Accords, made a last push toward the end of his presidency to negotiate peace between Israel and the Palestinians. He invited Israel's prime minister, Ehud Barak, to meet with Arafat at Camp David to resolve all open issues. According to Clinton, he got for Arafat everything he wanted. Nonetheless, Arafat rejected the deal, and the Second Intifada began.

The Second Intifada was far more violent than the first one. It lasted more than four years and resulted in the death of more than one thousand Israelis through suicide bombs, shootings, stone throwing, and rocket attacks. More than three thousand Palestinians died as well as a result of this revolt.

When President Bush took office in early 2001, he also sought to engage in Israel-Palestinian peacemaking. By this time, Israel was convinced that Arafat's representations to the United States regarding his peaceful intentions were lies. Two years later, Israel proved its contentions to be true. Its navy intercepted a Palestinian ship in the Red Sea called the *Karine A*, bound for Gaza. The ship contained Katyusha rockets, mortar shells, anti-tank missiles and mines, AK-47 assault rifles, explosives, and ammunition—all this bound for the PLO, which had committed to be demilitarized!

The *Karine A* affair ended Arafat's credibility with the United States. President Bush wrote in his memoir, "Arafat Lied to me. I never trusted him again." Arafat died two years later in 2004.

Mahmoud Abbas succeeded to the presidency of the Palestinian Authority and the chairmanship of the PLO, positions he still holds today. He was elected president in 2005 for four years. He has not convened an election since. He is referred to as being in the nineteenth year of a four-year term.

Abbas appears less threatening than Arafat, wearing business suits rather than Arafat's keffiyeh, military fatigues, and sidearm. But he is every bit as vile. On May 1, 2018, he spoke before the Palestinian National Congress and said that Jews had brought the Holocaust upon themselves by unscrupulous business dealings. It was a theme that he had raised many times before and continues to espouse today. So offensive was this remark that even the *New York Times*, perhaps the premier publication among Palestinian apologists, wrote an editorial the next day titled "Let Abbas's Vile Words Be His Last as Palestinian Leader." Nonetheless, Abbas continues in office and the world continues to treat him as a respected leader, including the *Times*.

I tweeted that day, as the U.S. ambassador to Israel, that Abbas had "reached a new low." I added, "To all those who think Israel is the reason we don't have peace, think again."

Shortly after Clinton and Barak failed to make a deal with Arafat in 2000, Ariel Sharon became the prime minister of Israel. He had a different approach to peacemaking. Rather than negotiate with a group of liars and antisemites, he thought it best for Israel simply to withdraw from the Gaza Strip, a territory where there were almost two million Palestinians and only nine thousand Jews. In August 2005, Sharon physically expelled all the Jews living in Gaza and withdrew Israel's military presence. The move was vehemently opposed by almost half the country.

Sharon approached President Bush before the expulsion, seeking assurances that if Israel left Gaza, it could at least retain parts of Judea and Samaria. On April 14, 2004, Bush wrote to Sharon, "In light of new realities on the ground . . . it is unrealistic to expect that the outcome of final status negotiations will be a full and complete return to the armistice lines of 1949."

The letter was hailed by Sharon as recognition that Israel could keep parts of Judea and Samaria. His celebration was premature. With the election of Barack Obama in 2008, incoming Secretary of State Hillary Clinton rejected Bush's words, finding all of Judea and Samaria to be illegally occupied by Israel.

The situation in Gaza deteriorated rapidly after Israel's withdrawal. The Palestinian Authority initially took control of Gaza upon Israel's disengagement, but in Gaza's first local election in 2006, Hamas, a terrorist organization designated as such by the United States and many other countries, emerged victorious. Hamas then took full control of the Gaza Strip by force in 2007.

A state of war between Israel and Hamas has existed ever since. In June 2006, Hamas kidnapped Israeli corporal Gilad Shalit, leading to the first of numerous Israeli defensive operations. Shalit later was released in an exchange for almost one thousand Palestinian prisoners, including Yahiya Sinwar who led the October 7 massacre.

In early 2008, Hamas began a practice that would continue to this day—firing rockets indiscriminately into Israeli population centers. Hamas could not control these rockets—they lacked any guidance mechanism. All Hamas could do was point the rockets in the direction of civilians and hope that they would kill as many as possible.

These rocket attacks have continued to the present and have included barrages of four hundred or more projectiles aimed at Israel's largest cities. Beginning in 2011, Israel began deploying its "Iron Dome" missile defense system, capable of shooting incoming rockets out of the sky. Even with this miraculous technology, some 10 percent of the rockets strike inside Israel with many unfortunate casualties over the years.

Many consider Iron Dome to be of great benefit to the Jewish state. In reality, the benefit runs more to the Palestinians. Without Iron Dome, Israel would have been required to resort to more conventional means of defense to arrest the incoming barrages. This, in turn, would have resulted in far more Palestinian casualties.

Many in the U.S. foreign policy establishment lament the takeover of Gaza by Hamas in 2007. They contend that things would have been different if the Palestinian Authority were in charge. I doubt it.

The Palestinian Authority is controlled by the PLO. The PLO was designated a terrorist organization by the United States in 1987, having committed atrocities against Israeli citizens every bit as callous as Hamas's. Nonetheless, presidential waivers have permitted U.S. officials to engage with PLO representatives continuously since 1988.

The Palestinian Authority is unique among governing authorities in its "pay for slay" program. This government-sponsored initiative compensates Palestinians who commit terror attacks against Jews—the more heinous the attack, the more Jews killed in the attack, the higher the compensation. The PA also generously compensates the families of terrorists who lose their lives in the course of committing an act of terrorism.

Palestinians receive more foreign aid per capita than any people on earth. Foreign aid to Palestinians between 1994 and 2020 totaled over forty billion dollars, a significant portion of which came from the United States. The United States will not give money directly to Gaza because it is controlled by Hamas. Instead, the United States funds the United Nations Relief and Works Agency (UNRWA), the only UN agency in the world dedicated to refugees from a single conflict. From 2014 to 2020, UN agencies—mostly UNRWA—spent about $4.5 billion in Gaza.

After the October 7, 2023, massacre by Hamas, it was revealed that a disturbing portion of UNRWA staff in Gaza were either Hamas terrorists, members, or sympathizers.

During the Trump administration, the United States cut off much of the Palestinians' direct and indirect U.S. funding, given their embrace of terror and disdain for peaceful coexistence. That spigot was turned back on with even greater force in the Biden administration.

What have the Palestinians done with all their financial assistance? In the first place, the leaders have pocketed it. Ismael Haniyah and Khalid Meshaal, the leaders of Hamas, are each said to be worth four billion dollars. They live like royalty in Qatar. Yasser Arafat's wife, Suha, is also said to be very rich. She lives in Paris and is often seen shopping in the expensive boutiques on the Champs-Élysées. And others within the upper echelons of the PA, the PLO, Hamas, and Islamic Jihad are also reported to have substantial bank accounts, including Mahmoud Abbas, who is said to be worth at least one hundred million dollars.

No Israeli prime minister has ever been reported to be worth even a fraction of Abbas's wealth. When I was the U.S. ambassador to Israel, I couldn't help but notice that the prime minister of Israel flew overseas in a commercial seat on a chartered El Al flight, while Abbas, whose territory had less than one twentieth of the GDP per capita of Israel, flew on a private Boeing Business Jet worth at least fifty million dollars.

When its leaders are not pocketing the foreign aid, Hamas is using its money to build missiles and a highly sophisticated web of terror tunnels. The web spans more than 350 miles in a territory that is only twenty-five miles long and six miles wide. This demonic infrastructure has given Hamas the greatest "home court advantage" in ground warfare, which it is deploying now in its war with Israel.

In short, the corruption and greed of the Palestinian leaders seems to know no bounds. But they have successfully extorted many nations to keep them flush with cash. There are many Palestinians around the world and many sympathizers who are hostile to Western values. Those nations that do not "pay the Palestinian piper" are likely to find internal protests and worse.

When I was in government, a Palestinian initiative called "Peace to Prosperity" was convened by my friend Jared Kushner in Manama, the capital city of Bahrain. The sole purpose of the conference was to consider how to fund infrastructure and educational development in Palestinian territories to reduce the friction and hostility that had emerged. Some of the largest investors in the world attended, including the CEO of Blackstone and many sovereign wealth funds. Only one party boycotted the event—the Palestinians.

Here was an event in which the world's wealthiest investors were present, with Palestinian prosperity the only agenda item, and Abbas prohibited Palestinians from attending. A single Palestinian businessman from Hebron who showed up was jailed by the PA upon his return.

Abbas's reaction to the conference was that it could "go to hell." His interest has never been the prosperity of his people. It's only about destroying Israel.

Which brings us to October 7, 2023, perhaps the culmination of all the Palestinian hatred and vitriol taught and developed by Palestinian leaders over decades. Hamas terrorists breached the southern border of Israel and went on a rampage in which 1,200 innocent men, women, and children—babies and grandmothers among them—were murdered, including many who were first raped, mutilated, and burned. Another 250 were taken hostage with over 116 remaining in captivity as of the day this book was completed. Tens of thousands of missiles were also launched into Israel by Hamas from the South and Hezbollah from the North.

Israel has fought back magnificently, employing extraordinary measures to avoid, wherever possible, civilian casualties. The percentage of Gaza civilians killed as a percentage of combatants killed is said by experts to be the lowest in modern warfare. Nonetheless, Hamas sympathizers abound in Judea and Samaria and throughout the world.

So let's finish this chapter where we began: Who are the Palestinians?

They are a people with no discernible religious, cultural, or territorial identity. Most live in Jordan, but many live all around the world.

They formed a national movement in 1964 with the goal of destroying Israel. Once they realized that was impossible, lip service was paid to peaceful coexistence, but it was never actualized. They have a repressive society, subjugating women and outlawing homosexuality. They have created no government institutions fostering human rights, transparency, or accountability.

They rejoice in the brutal murder of Jews, a disturbing phenomenon we have seen quite recently. Americans might also recall that they rejoiced after the terror attacks of September 11, 2001.

They undoubtedly include good, hardworking, well-meaning people who do not wish harm on anyone else. I have met these people. But they are drowned out by their malign leaders.

Many will say that they are living substandard existences and have a right to anger. Maybe, but not against Israel. Beginning in 1947 and continuing through 2000, Israel has made generous—I would argue too generous, bordering on sacrificial—offers to live in peace with the Palestinians. All have been rejected. If Palestinians are suffering, and many are not, the fault lies with their leadership.

In all of modern Israel's history, there has never been a Jewish movement to expel Arabs or any other minority from the land of Israel. Israel was created upon a platform of coexistence, and it continues that goal today, even in the aftermath of October 7. In contrast, there never has been a Palestinian movement for coexistence—there have occasionally been platitudes offered in this direction, but no Palestinian leader has ever engaged in a process of real peace. Indeed, Palestinian leaders routinely demand the expulsion of every Jew as part of their Palestinian state fantasy. They also backchannel messaging to their local audience that they have never abandoned the goal of Israel's destruction.

Under no circumstances do the Palestinians merit, nor could they justify, a second Palestinian state in addition to Jordan.

6
LAND FOR PEACE /
LAND FOR TERROR

How often has a nation been attacked, come back to defeat its enemy, capture territory in aid of its security, and then give the captured territory back? The answer is almost never, one notable exception being Israel's return of the Sinai Peninsula to Egypt as part of a 1978 peace treaty called the Camp David Accords. That return constituted more than 80 percent of the territory Israel captured in the Six-Day War of 1967.

The land captured by Israel in the Six-Day War was indeed achieved within a defensive battle. It began with Egypt blocking the Straits of Tiran—a passageway essential for shipments into Israel's Port of Eilat—and amassing a large number of troops along the border. In response, Israel launched an airstrike against Egypt and then responded to Jordan, Syria, and Lebanon as they entered the war.

"Land for peace" is such a simple concept that many think it happens often in the course of bilateral dispute resolutions. Just the opposite. Victorious nations have no interest in granting back land to an aggressor that attacked them without justification. The reasons are obvious: First, the granting country would be giving up tangible territory in exchange for a naked promise of peace, creating a distinct lack of symmetry. Second, the granting country, having been attacked and having responded successfully in a defensive war, justifiably will want to impose some territorial cost on its adversary for its invasion. Asking a country that was attacked to then reward its attacker, not surprisingly, is a tough sell.

Nonetheless, in 2011 President Barack Obama announced that Israel should give back just about all of Judea and Samaria in order to achieve peace with the Palestinians—a group of people who never had a national presence in that territory or elsewhere. Indeed, the Kingdom of Jordan, the existing Palestinian state that occupied Judea and Samaria from 1948 until 1967, renounced its claim to the territory pursuant to its peace treaty with Israel in 1994.

We know, with certainty, that land-for-peace deals involving Israel don't work. We know that because Israel has, in the past, endeavored to achieve peace on this basis without success. It began with southern Lebanon, extended to Area A in Judea and Samaria, and of course, reached its nadir in Gaza. Even in the case of Egypt, subject to a successful and (to date) enduring peace treaty with Israel, when Israel left the Sinai Peninsula, the vacuum created was filled by ISIS and other terror groups. Israel assisted Egypt in defending itself against ISIS.

Israel undertook a land-for-peace experiment in 2005 with its withdrawal from Gaza. It left Gaza barren of Jews and without an Israeli military presence. The Palestinians in Gaza were then given billions of dollars of foreign aid to build their Palestinian state. It could have been quite a successful state with a lengthy western-facing border along the Mediterranean Sea. The land was beautiful, the climate exceptional, and the opportunities enormous. But with Hamas's takeover of Gaza in 2007, the foreign aid did not go to commerce, education, or health care. Instead, it went to rockets, missiles, and the largest network of terror tunnels in the world.

The consequences of Israel ceding control of Gaza are heartbreaking: rocket attacks, suicide bombs, death, and property destruction every year since 2007, culminating on October 7, 2023, in the worst assault against the Jewish people since the Holocaust.

In response to the October 7 atrocities, the Biden administration has implored Israel to implement a "two-state solution" to restore peace to the region. How tone-deaf! The very practice that created the Palestinian terror state in Gaza is one that Biden seeks to repeat. The Gaza experiment proves, with certainty, that a two-state solution is simply a suicidal formula to create a terror state.

The failure of the Oslo Accords supports the same conclusion. Under Oslo, Israel ceded military and civilian control of "Area A"—about 20 percent of Judea and Samaria—to the Palestinian Authority. Another 20 percent, referred to as Area B, is subject to Palestinian civilian control and Israeli military control. Included within Area A are the Palestinian cities of Jenin, Tulkarm, Nablus, and Ramallah—all hotbeds of Palestinian violence notwithstanding the absence of an Israeli presence. Israelis are prohibited from entering Areas A and B.

From cities in Area A, many hundreds of terror attacks have been inflicted on Israelis living both inside the Green Line and in Area C—the section of Judea and

Samaria where Jews live. The number of casualties since 1993 is in the tens of thousands.

Whenever Israel cedes territory to Palestinians, the territory becomes a breeding ground and launching pad for terrorists.

This lesson also could have been learned from the first and second Lebanon wars. In 1982, Israel went into Lebanon to end the steady stream of attacks by Lebanese terror groups, including the PLO, on Israelis living in the north. In 1985, Israel pulled back to a buffer zone, where it remained until 2000. Israel then drew back to its northern border, creating a vacuum that was soon filled by Hezbollah, an Iran-sponsored Shiite terror group.

By 2006, Hezbollah launched an attack on Israel leading to a war that lasted thirty-four days. It conducted a cross-border raid where it ambushed and killed three Israeli soldiers. The war ended with the United Nations Security Council passing resolution 1701, which called upon Hezbollah to disarm and empowered UNIFIL—the United Nations Interim Force in Lebanon—to ensure that Hezbollah remained disarmed. UNIFIL did such a horrendous job that Hezbollah is now the second most powerful military in the Middle East, behind only Israel. Hezbollah, which had only a few thousand primitive missiles in 2006, today has highly sophisticated weaponry, including almost one hundred thousand precision guided missiles.

The lessons of Israel's withdrawal from Gaza, southern Lebanon, and parts of Judea and Samaria are the same: First, giving away land in exchange for a promise of peace from disreputable and hateful parties is a fool's errand and recklessly irresponsible to Israel's citizens. Second, the probability that the PLO, the United Nations, or other parties will police the territory surrendered by

Israel is essentially zero. History tells us that it is a certainty that when Israel walks away from territory, the results are nothing short of a national nightmare.

Left-wing politicians in the United States, Israel and elsewhere, speak with deep conviction of the need for a two-state solution to the Israeli-Palestinian conflict. They fantasize of two peoples living side by side in peace and harmony. The problem is that one of those two peoples has leadership, and many inhabitants, who instead want to destroy Israel by fomenting war and terror.

One U.S. senator once criticized my skepticism regarding a two-state solution, convinced that such an outcome was essential in enabling Israel to remain both Jewish and a democracy. I responded that those were pretty high-class concerns for a single Jewish state surrounded by hostile and violent Arabs. I suggested that before getting to "Jewish and Democratic," we prioritize the need to "be alive and survive." Until that can be guaranteed, all the hypothetical plans and fantasies are not relevant.

7

CHURCH AND STATE: DO THEY MIX?

Few provisions of the U.S. Constitution are more well known or garner more approval than the religious freedom clauses of the First Amendment: "Congress shall make no law respecting an establishment of religion, or prohibiting the free exercise thereof."

The United States was designed as a religiously neutral republic. There was to be no official religion, nor were there to be impediments to religious observance.

But religiously neutral does not mean irreligious. Indeed, the words "In God We Trust" are the official motto of the United States and have withstood constitutional challenges in numerous federal appellate courts. You would be hard-pressed to find a federal government building or an item of U.S. currency that does not bear this motto.

Notwithstanding the words of our Constitution, it is the word of God that has had the greatest and most beneficial impact on our nation. The Declaration of Independence recognized, for the first time since the Bible itself, that human rights were not granted by the sovereign but rather endowed BY GOD in every human life. As stated in this watershed document, "life, liberty and the pursuit of happiness" are all rights "endowed by our Creator." That was an earthquake of an idea—human rights are derived from God, making those rights nonnegotiable, absolute, and immutable.

How did the United States' Founding Fathers arrive at a basket of human rights that they determined to be endowed by God? After all, there are literally hundreds of "rights" one might imagine, many of which have been asserted over the years. But "life, liberty and the pursuit of happiness" were the rights specifically enumerated. The answer is simple: the United States' founders were Bible scholars, and these rights are plainly set forth in the divine text of the Old Testament:

> Life: "and you shall choose life"—Deuteronomy 30:19
>
> Liberty: "and you shall proclaim Liberty throughout the land"—Leviticus 25:10 (a phrase inscribed on the Liberty Bell some fifty years before the Declaration of Independence was signed)
>
> Happiness: "and you shall be happy with all the good given to you by God"—Deuteronomy 26:11

The United States' relationship with God is thus a bit complicated. There is no official religion, and yet there also is no denying the seminal role of God in our society. Christians make up about 63 percent of the U.S. population, a number that has shrunk over the decades as the "no religion" category has grown. Even as it has grown smaller, however, Christianity remains the dominant religion in the United States. Indeed, Christmas Day, Good

Friday, and Easter are all national holidays. Nonetheless, the First Amendment ensures that other religions are not materially disadvantaged.

While the First Amendment has played an essential role in the development of the United States, many other countries have gone in a different direction. The United Kingdom, for example, from which the United States was spawned, considers the Anglican Church, also referred to as the Church of England, to be its state religion. That doesn't mean that non-Anglicans suffer in England, either in terms of their human rights or their freedom of worship. But it does mean that the United Kingdom has preserved its historical faith as foundational to its existence. Anyone who has recently observed the investiture of King Charles could not help but appreciate how deeply the Anglican Church is infused within official government affairs.

Most nations with a state-sponsored religion are located in or around the Middle East, and the religion is Islam. Here's a list of official Muslim countries—this doesn't even include nations where Islam is the "preferred" but not "official" religion:

Afghanistan	Jordan
Algeria	Kuwait
Bahrain	Libya
Bangladesh	Malaysia
Brunei	Maldives
Comoros	Mauritania
Djibouti	Morocco
Egypt	Oman
Iran	Pakistan
Iraq	Qatar

Saudi Arabia   Western Sahara
Somalia   Yemen
United Arab Emirates

There are thus twenty-five countries for which Islam is the official state religion. Again, we are excluding nations like Syria, Lebanon, and Tunisia, which clearly have a Muslim character but don't name Islam as their state religion in their governing documents.

In some of these countries, one would be very uncomfortable if not a member of the Muslim faith. In others, for example, Saudi Arabia and the Emirates, there are thousands of Western expatriates living in those countries who feel welcome and lead successful and fulfilling lives.

My point is not to advocate for or against a nation having a national religion. In some cases, it unites the inhabitants of the country in the same way as cultural or linguistic commonalities. In other cases, a national religion can have an exclusionary effect on minorities, if there are any.

But if these twenty-five countries in and around the Middle East can have a specific attachment to a particular religion—with absolutely no one in the international community being heard to complain—certainly the same can be true of the one Jewish state: the State of Israel. This especially is true given that Judaism is the only religion that also is a nationality.

Israel's status as a Jewish state is more precisely defined and circumscribed than most of the twenty-five countries listed above. In the first instance, Judaism is not the official religion of Israel. Although 75 percent of the country is Jewish and the holidays and national events mostly follow the Jewish calendar, it would be more accurate to say that Israel is the nation-state of the Jewish people.

Israel's connection to the Jewish people was established on the day it was founded, May 14, 1948. The preamble to its Declaration of Independence states in part,

> The Land of Israel was the birthplace of the Jewish people. Here their spiritual, religious and political identity was shaped. Here they first attained to statehood, created cultural values of national and universal significance and gave it to the world in the eternal Book of Books.

The declaration then goes on to "declare the establishment of a Jewish state in Eretz-Israel to be known as the State of Israel."

Israel's Declaration of Independence created a careful balance between the foundation of a Jewish state and the rights of the state's inhabitants who are not Jewish. Its language is inspiring:

> The State of Israel will be open for Jewish immigration and for the Ingathering of the Exiles; it will foster the development of the country for the benefit of all its inhabitants; it will be based on freedom, justice and peace as envisaged by the prophets of Israel; it will ensure complete equality of social and political rights to all its inhabitants irrespective of religion, race or sex; it will guarantee freedom of religion, conscience, language, education and culture; it will safeguard the Holy Places of all religions and it will be faithful to the principles of the charter of the United Nations.

Israel's founding was as welcoming an invitation as one could draft to live in peace and harmony with its neighbors. It didn't matter. It contrasts starkly with both the PLO and Hamas charters, which call for Israel's elimination.

Israel's conciliatory language mattered little to its neighbors: Five Arab nations attacked Israel the day after the Declaration of Independence was issued.

Israel has continued ever since its founding to thread the needle between the primacy of the rights of the Jewish people to their biblical homeland and the recognition that Israel must protect the human and civil rights of all its inhabitants, including its minorities.

Israel does not have a constitution, but its Knesset (parliament) does pass "Basic laws" that have quasi-constitutional authority. Since its inception, Israel has struggled with what it means to be a Jewish state while at the same time being a democracy. It has scrupulously sought to preserve the religious, social, and political rights of its minority population—about 20 percent of the population, most of which is Arab—at a time when many within its minority were hostile to the state.

These efforts occurred over decades within the backdrop of wars, intifadas, and mass terror attacks. One might hypothesize what another country might do to a minority population at a time when the majority is under attack by enemies ethnically aligned with the minority. We can look inward at how the United States mistreated its Japanese citizens in World War II as an example of how things can go wrong when fears, tensions, and emotions are inflamed.

Israel didn't go there. After Israel's War of Independence in 1948, about 156,000 Arabs lived inside the country. That number has increased to over two million Arabs today. Similarly, there were 265,000 Palestinians living in Gaza in 1948. Today there are over two million.

But the statistics are even more compelling when one considers the ethnic cleansing of the Jews from Arab lands:

In 1948, the Jewish population in Morocco was 265,000. In 2023 it was 2,000.

In 1948, the Jewish population in Algeria was 140,000. In 2023 it was 50.

In 1948, the Jewish population in Tunisia was 150,000. In 2023 it was 50.

In 1948, the Jewish population in Libya was 38,000. In 2023 it was zero.

In 1948, the Jewish population in Egypt was 75,000. In 2023, it was 40.

In 1948, the Jewish population in Yemen was 55,000. In 2023 it was 50.

In 1948, the Jewish population in Iraq was 150,000. In 2023 it was 7.

In 1948, the Jewish population in Syria was 40,000. In 2023 it was zero.

In 1948, the Jewish population in Lebanon was 20,000. In 2023 it was 100.

I suppose I could have put these numbers in one big chart and saved a page. But each of the prior paragraphs represents far more than a number. It represents real people unceremoniously expelled from Arab lands with not much more than the shirts on their backs. Even those who had accumulated significant wealth were forced to forfeit everything for which they and their families had worked for generations.

Many of the Jewish refugees from these Arab lands—children at the time—are still around today and remember the stressful challenges of their early years. While UNRWA was supporting the Palestinians, neither the UN nor any nation other than Israel was helping these Jewish refugees. To this day, none of the 930,000 expelled Jews have been compensated for their losses. And the world could not care less.

To put this in the starkest terms, since 1948, the Jewish population in Arab countries has been reduced by 99.83 percent. In contrast, the Arab population in Israel has increased by 1,296 percent—far more than tenfold.

For the world to accuse Israel now of genocide is grotesque and maliciously false. The fact that any university, with its access to an abundance of research and data, permits these accusations by its students with no attempt to correct the record is just shameful.

There is another reason why it is exceptionally painful to hear misinformed students on college campuses accuse Israel of genocide—an accusation that has even reached the halls of Congress among hateful representatives. It is painful because the State of Israel came into existence when real genocide—Hitler's plan to exterminate the Jews—was fresh in the minds of the Israeli pioneers. It was something that the Jewish people, more than any other people on earth, took pains to make sure was never repeated. And indeed, they succeeded in protecting their minorities, even in times of war and incitement. Wherever Israel has controlled territory, its Arab population has skyrocketed, at a rate higher than even that of the Jews.

In 1992, Israel took huge steps to codify the rights of its minority. It passed "Basic Law: Human Dignity and Liberty," a law designed to protect the human rights of every citizen. The law recognized entitlements to personal liberty and freedom of movement, religion, expression, creativity, and privacy as constitutional rights. In 1994, the law was amended to establish the constitutional status of the aspirations expressed in the Declaration of Independence.

These were the halcyon days of the Israeli peace movement, with Israel signing a peace treaty with Jordan and Prime Minister Yitzchak Rabin leading a skeptical nation into the Oslo Accords, all with the charismatic encouragement of President Clinton. But the Palestinians were on a different page, unable or unwilling to control the continuous onslaught of terror attacks against Israeli civilians. By 1995, Prime Minister Rabin was killed by a Jewish assassin, and a year later, the Israeli right pulled off a narrow but stunning electoral victory led by Benjamin Netanyahu.

The Basic Law of Human Dignity was unassailable as a step forward for human rights. But to many it reflected a swing of the pendulum too far to the left—to the point of creating universal rights untethered to Judaism or the Jewish people. While many on the Israeli left wanted a carbon copy of the U.S. model, there was that nagging issue of where Judaism was to fit in.

The pendulum swung back on July 19, 2018, when the Knesset passed "Basic Law: Israel as the Nation-State of the Jewish People," commonly referred to as the "Nation-State Law." It was more than twenty years in coming and reflected a backlash against the small but powerful "post-Zionism" elements within Israeli society and Israel critics around the world. Under the guise of saving "democracy," many critics, including large American Jewish organizations, opposed the Nation-State Law precisely because it formalized the irrevocable connection of Israel to the Jewish people.

For decades, the anti-Israel movements saw the path to Israel's demise running through the delegitimization of its ancient history. This took numerous forms, including the passage in 2017 by UNESCO—the UN's cultural body—of a resolution on "Occupied Palestine" stating that Israel had no legal or historical rights anywhere in Jerusalem. This in turn came on the heels of the United States permitting passage of United Nations Security Council Resolution 2334, a resolution that found Israel to have no legal rights to its biblical homeland in Judea and Samaria. I have referred to this resolution on many occasions as the greatest betrayal of Israel by a U.S. president (Obama) in history.

These resolutions simply institutionalized the Palestinian narrative that they, not the Jews, were the real ancient people of the land of Israel. In our "post-truth" society, where outright lies are shamelessly introduced into the public square and then embraced by those whose agenda fits the narrative, it is not surprising that the Palestinian lies found a home.

Of course, the Palestinians often self-destruct, even in their completely contrived national narrative. Not wanting to offend the Christian world, which is even larger than that of Islam, they acknowledged that while Jews were devoid of any connection to Jerusalem, Christians were different. That self-defeating argument, which Palestinians continue to espouse, cannot be true, since the Christian connection to Jerusalem stems from Jesus's preaching and ultimate crucifixion in Jerusalem, which Jesus experienced as a Jew!

The Nation-State Law was enacted to make it abundantly clear that Israel was a Jewish state. The primary provisions of this law include the following:

1. A declaration that the land of Israel is the historical homeland of the Jewish people.
2. A declaration that the right to exercise national self-determination in the State of Israel is unique to the Jewish people.
3. A declaration that Jerusalem, complete and united, is the capital of Israel.
4. The state will strive to protect Jews anywhere that they are in peril because of their Jewishness or their citizenship.
5. The development of Jewish settlement in Israel was viewed as a national value.
6. National symbols such as the Star of David, Menorah, the national anthem, and Hatikva were recognized, along with Hebrew as the official language (providing "special status" to the Arabic language).

Prime Minister Netanyahu oversaw the passage of the Nation-State Law. Upon its passage, he declared triumphantly:

This is our country, the state of the Jews, but in recent years, there are those who try to undermine this and to undermine the foundation of our existence and rights. And today, we have legislated into the foundation of the law—this is our state. This is our language. This is our anthem. This is our flag. Long live Israel.

I remember sitting in my office in Jerusalem on July 19, 2018, when the Nation-State Law was enacted by the Knesset. It was just about two months after I had presided over the moving of the United States embassy from Tel Aviv to Jerusalem. Calls were coming into the White House from various nations and groups of nations, especially from the Muslim world, complaining that the Nation-State Law was racist. For example, the Organization of Islamic Cooperation (OIC) issued a statement that the law "ignores the historical rights of the Palestinians, both Muslim and Christian, and represents an extension to the Israeli settlement ideology and occupation policies, based on ethnic cleansing and denial of the existence of Palestinian people and history, highlighted by international resolutions."

More than fifty Muslim nations make up the OIC, all bound together because of their common national faith. I found it very ironic that this religious group couldn't see room in the world for a single Jewish state in the land promised to the Jews by God in a text considered by the Muslim faith to be sacred.

I got several calls that day from U.S. officials in the State Department and the White House. They in turn were hearing not only from the OIC but also from the European Union and other countries traditionally hostile to Israel criticizing the law. More important were the incoming calls from U.S. leaders on the left, especially Jewish ones, complaining that this flawed legislation would hamper peace negotiations (not that there were any at that time) and was the result of the United States emboldening Israel by moving the U.S. embassy. I was asked how the United States should respond.

My response was simple. The United States need not respond. This was an internal decision by the Israeli government to reinforce Israel's status as a Jewish state, a fact that is not subject to debate.

Notwithstanding my advice, someone in the U.S. government leaked that the United States was "concerned" that the Nation-State Law would adversely affect Israel's minorities. On August 1, 2018, I met with Prime Minister Netanyahu on other matters. At that meeting he clarified to me that there would be no adverse effect. I passed that on to the White House, and there was never any public criticism of the law by any U.S. foreign policy official.

The Nation-State Law was challenged by numerous litigants before the Israeli Supreme Court. The court, considered left-leaning and of an activist nature by many, agreed that all eleven members of the court would hear the appeal, a sign of how significant the issues were.

In July 2021, the Israeli Supreme Court, by a vote of 10–1, upheld the validity of the Nation-State Law, stating that the "Basic Law is but one chapter in our constitution taking shape and it does not negate Israel's character as a democratic state." The court's theory was that individual human rights were not affected by the law—indeed those were now well-established by the Basic Law on Human Dignity. The law's primary declaration that "national rights"—that is, the national right to self-determination—would be reserved to the Jewish people was not undemocratic.

Considering the Basic Law of Human Dignity together with the Nation-State Law demonstrates that the architecture of Israeli legislation provides sufficient flexibility for two salutary outcomes to be achieved simultaneously: (1) the grant of the right of human dignity—extrapolated to include freedoms of expression, movement, worship, and occupation—to every inhabitant of Israel and (2) the grant of the collective national right of self-determination exclusively to the Jewish people, ensuring Israel's permanency as a Jewish state.

Is enshrining a national religious character in a nation unusual? It's certainly not the U.S. model. But it is the rule rather than the exception in the Middle East.

Other democratic countries have also codified their national character. My friend Professor Eugene Kontorovich points to Latvia, Slovakia, and Slovenia, democracies that emerged from the breakup of the Soviet Union and Yugoslavia, as good examples of this development. In *A Comparative Constitutional Perspective on Israel's Nation-State Law* (2020), he writes,

> The Latvian constitution opens by invoking the "unwavering will of the Latvian nation to have its own State and its inalienable right of self-determination to guarantee the existence and development of the Latvian nation, its language and culture throughout the centuries. . . ." In any reading of these provisions, the "nation" cannot be understood as referring simply to the totality of its citizens. The "nation" is separate from its citizens and dependent upon ethnicity. (p. 143)

Kontorovich provides similar illustrations with regard to Slovakia and Slovenia. While none of these are perfect analogs to Israel, a law recognizing the primacy of the ancient religious and national history of the Jewish people—as reflected in the Nation-State Law—would seem far less controversial than the constitutional protection afforded by these countries to a far less defined national culture.

We can conclude this analysis as follows: While Church and State are largely separated in the U.S. democracy, other democracies, especially those whose societies are bound together by a strong common ethnicity and/or religion, have successfully granted special rights to collective national self-determination to its foundational majority, while still ensuring the human rights of its minority. And lots of other countries that are not democracies do the same in a far more pronounced way with no one batting an eye.

To understand better how this balancing might be applied to Israel and Judea and Samaria, we need to understand a Caribbean Island some six thousand miles away—Puerto Rico.

8

THE WEALTHY PORT

Puerto Rico, meaning the "Wealthy Port" in Spanish, was acquired by the United States in 1898 under the provisions of the Treaty of Paris, which ended the Spanish-American War. In 1917, Puerto Rico was designated an unincorporated United States territory, and its residents became United States citizens soon thereafter.

The means by which Puerto Rico was integrated into the United States and the judicial and legislative architecture by which its inhabitants gained legal rights provide important data points for a resolution of issues relating to Judea and Samaria. Today, the residents of Puerto Rico do not vote in U.S. national elections. They do, however, benefit from well-recognized human rights and elect their civilian leaders. While not a perfect analogy to Israel, Puerto Rico ensures the human dignity of its citizens while foregoing collective national rights, resolving, just as Israel must do, the tension between these two doctrines. And the United States maintains full sovereignty over Puerto Rico. It all seems to work.

Puerto Rico's history is illuminating. From 1901 until 1950, it was operated in accordance with a series of

Supreme Court decisions known as the "Insular Cases," referring to the fact that Puerto Rico was governed by the U.S. War Department's Bureau of Insular Affairs.

The Insular Cases reflected the thinking within the United States at the time. The decisions represented an endorsement of U.S. "empire building" and have in recent years been labeled racist. I am not endorsing following the approach of these cases but rather referring to them to illustrate how the United States' position on Puerto Rico evolved to a place that is a "win-win" outcome for all.

In the earliest of the Insular Cases, the Supreme Court held that the residents of Puerto Rico were not entitled to the protections of the U.S. Constitution. They were found to be entitled to some undefined "fundamental rights," but certainly not the Bill of Rights.

The issue was revisited again in 1922 after the residents of Puerto Rico were granted U.S. citizenship. A Puerto Rican resident challenged his denial of a trial by jury, a basic U.S. constitutional right. Again, notwithstanding his U.S. citizenship, the Supreme Court held that the constitutional right was not available.

These decisions left many Americans uncomfortable. On the one hand, many agreed that the United States did not need to treat those living in an unincorporated territory in the same manner as those inside the United States. But at the same time, if the residents of Puerto Rico could not gain the benefits of the U.S. Constitution's framework for civil and human rights, shouldn't they have the ability to choose for themselves the rights to which they would be entitled?

This sentiment gained acceptance, and in 1950 Congress passed legislation authorizing the residents of Puerto Rico to write a constitution to govern themselves. They passed such a constitution in 1952, which largely mirrored that of the United States and created three similar branches of government. This development had a significant impact with regard to how the Supreme Court dealt with Puerto Rico from then on.

In the 1975 case of *Torres v. Puerto Rico*, a criminal defendant got off a flight from the United States to San Juan, had his baggage checked without cause or a search warrant, and illegal substances were found. The search was permitted under the local laws of Puerto Rico. The U.S. Supreme Court, however, reversed the defendant's conviction, finding that the search and seizure violated Puerto Rico's constitution, which federal courts were now bound to enforce. The people of Puerto Rico were now gaining the civil rights they had been denied years earlier.

This brings us to the modern era. In 2022, yet another challenge was made to the disparate treatment between U.S. citizens residing in Puerto Rico and those residing within the fifty states. In *United States v. Vaello Madero*, the issue at hand was whether a Puerto Rican resident could be excluded from the Supplemental Security Income Program available to residents of the states. In an 8–1 majority opinion, the Supreme Court held that residents of Puerto Rico, even though citizens, could be treated differently under the laws of the United States. As an example of why this was justified, the court noted that residents of Puerto Rico, even though U.S. citizens, do not pay certain federal taxes, and therefore it was not unfair to deny them certain federal benefits.

To this day, the law, properly evolving over time to ensure fairness to Puerto Rican residents, nonetheless retains two features: (1) the United States has absolute sovereignty over Puerto Rico, and (2) the people of Puerto Rico have extensive rights of self-government but not collective national rights to vote in U.S. elections. It is a formula within which both the United States and Puerto have moved forward in peace and prosperity. No one has seriously accused the United States of being an apartheid state by reason of this construct.

Why does it work? In the 1970s and 1980s there was a Puerto Rican nationalist movement called the FALN—Fuerzas Armadas de Liberación Nacional (Armed Forces of National Liberation)—which engaged in significant terror activities in the United States in its quest for Puerto Rican independence. But no more. Why? Why is there no protest or violence on account of the fact that Puerto Rican citizens lack national suffrage?

The simple answer is that the bilateral relationship works. The people of Puerto Rico live better lives as an unincorporated territory of the United States than they would if independent. Puerto Rico is situated in a region subject to hurricanes and other natural disasters. With regard just to those risks, as of June 2023, FEMA—the Federal Emergency Management Agency—has awarded $23.4 billion in public assistance for Puerto Rico to recover from its 2017 hurricanes and 2019 and 2020 earthquakes.

We all recall the famous cry that animated the American Revolution, "no taxation without representation." Perhaps that is a legitimate complaint elsewhere, but not in Puerto Rico. U.S. citizens residing in Puerto Rico do not pay full federal income taxes. Of course, they do pay taxes to the Commonwealth of Puerto Rico, but they have the right to vote for the executives and legislators of the commonwealth.

Puerto Rico has saved us all the heavy lifting in crafting a Jewish state with sovereignty over Palestinian communities in Judea and Samaria. We can skip all the methods that failed or were branded colonial or racist. Let's just go straight to the principles endorsed by eight out of nine Supreme Court justices of the United States.

First, absolute Israeli sovereignty over all Judea and Samaria.

Second, Palestinians within Judea and Samaria should have all the civil and human rights called for by Israel's Basic Law on Human Dignity, without the collective right to self-determination as provided in the Nation-State Law. In other words, Palestinians, like Puerto Ricans, will not vote in national elections.

Third, Palestinians will be free to enact their own governing documents, as long as they are not inconsistent with those of Israel.

Fourth, Palestinians will not pay Israeli income taxes but will be taxed to support their local needs. Palestinians, just as Puerto Ricans, will give less to their sovereign nation and receive less in return. As Arab Israelis currently do not serve in the Israeli military, the same would apply to Arabs living in Judea and Samaria. Perhaps that will evolve over time.

Why would this ultimately make sense for Palestinians? For the same reason that Puerto Rico is willing to accept fewer national rights in exchange for U.S. aid and protections like FEMA. Israel is the only nation that can bring the Palestinians into the twenty-first century.

Some will consider the following analogy inapposite, but I think it's appropriate. There are some major companies traded on the national stock exchanges with two classes of voting stock: Class A, which has voting control of the company, and Class B, which does not. Otherwise, the two classes of stock have identical rights to the assets and earnings of the company. Usually, the nonvoting stock trades at a small discount to the voting stock—all things being equal, one would pay slightly more to be able to vote his or her shares. But only slightly more.

For many investors, the Class B shares are a better buy. They are not particularly interested in changing the board of the company or otherwise engaging in corporate governance. What they want is to get their share if the company is sold or pays a dividend—and they get that at a cheaper price than the voting shares.

People affirmatively make these types of decisions every day. And it would be entirely rational and appropriate for the Palestinians in Judea and Samaria to accept the "discount" of not voting in a national election if they receive benefits otherwise unattainable.

In the United States, we also have two means of caring for orphans and abused children: adoption and foster parenting. Living in the same home, there could be one kid who has been adopted and another who is there as a foster child. Obviously, from the child's perspective, it's better to be adopted. It creates more stability and permanence. And there may indeed be tension between the adopted child and the foster care child because of the difference in status. But no one has suggested eliminating the foster parent program—it's still far better than forcing a child to live in an abusive environment.

I am not analogizing Palestinians in Judea and Samaria to foster children. What I am saying is that not every instance of disparate treatment inside a society is discriminatory or condemnable. Some, of course, are: forcing one ethnic group to attend segregated schools or occupy segregated facilities solely based on race or ethnicity is outrageous and thankfully gone from the United States, Israel, and most other democracies. But attempting to integrate within society a group dominated for years by hostile forces is an enormous and unprecedented challenge, and we can't let the perfect undermine the possible. Living as permanent residents of Judea and Samaria under Israeli rule is a massively better option for Palestinians than living in the abusive conditions created by the PLO and Hamas.

Arab Israeli citizens serving in the Knesset have shown little interest in engaging in national affairs. As representatives of a minority, they have focused on ensuring that their constituency is treated fairly in specific matters that affect them directly. In Judea and Samaria, Palestinians should certainly have the right to benefit from leaders who would do the same.

With appropriate and necessary security assurances and financial assistance, Israel alone can work with Palestinian civilian leadership to bring the Palestinian economy, educational system, and health care programs up to first-world standards. The Palestinians know that, perhaps better than anyone. Liberated from their corrupt leadership, they can begin to abandon their narrative of victimization and move forward with peace, dignity, and prosperity.

9
WHAT'S LAW GOT TO DO WITH IT?

I practiced law for thirty-five years. I have great respect for the law and for the need to live within a rules-based society. History has shown us that human beings left to their own proclivities of greed, self-preservation, and self-rationalization can get to a pretty dark place without a system of laws and a judicial system capable of fairly enforcing them.

One of the great features of the American republic is an independent judiciary with federal judges serving life terms and thus unbeholden to the whims of politics. Faith in the fairness of our judicial system—in the blindness of justice—is an essential component in the stability of our society.

Lately, that faith has taken an enormous hit with the prosecution—and in one absurd New York State case, the conviction—of former president and current candidate Donald Trump. Even if the cases had merit, as some incorrectly believe, the timing of four criminal prosecutions all brought in proximity to a federal election cannot escape the stench of a political conspiracy by the Democratic Party to keep a popular opposing candidate off the ballot. A deep dive into the cases, which we will not do here, makes that conclusion inescapable.

We must repair our U.S. judicial system to restore the confidence in it of the American people. But as to the world of "international law," it is already broken and beyond repair.

Critics of Israel often accuse it of violating international law. They almost never point to specific violations or raise supporting facts. Because they can't.

The laws of warfare generally arise from the 1949 Geneva Conventions, which sought, unsuccessfully, to establish rules to prevent another Holocaust. Since 1949, there have been countless violators of these rules, including Russia, China, Cambodia, and numerous warring parties in Africa and Asia. Why aren't the rules effective? Because the people violating these rules don't care about breaking the law!

The rules of warfare are fairly straightforward and intuitive: no torture, rape, executions, or targeting of civilians. And if you target an enemy that is embedded among civilians, you should use reasonable efforts to minimize the civilian casualties subject to the overriding goal of defeating the enemy.

In its war against Hamas in Gaza that began October 7, 2023, Israel confronted an army with the greatest "home court advantage" in the history of modern warfare—a 350-mile network of concrete-reinforced terror tunnels equipped with ventilation, command and control equipment, and stockpiles of weapons and all necessities. It was an army with offensive capabilities installed in hospitals and schools. And it was an army that initially held 250 soldiers and civilians captive.

With the benefit of six months of statistics related to the battle, even using the casualty figures from the "Gaza Health Ministry," which undoubtedly are inflated, it is clear that Israel has killed fewer civilians in relation to Gaza combatants than in any other war in modern history. Israel bends over backward to comply with the laws of warfare, both because it is the right thing to do and because, given the diplomatic fallout it endures from almost all the nations of the world, it is in its national interests to minimize civilian deaths.

When the war began, Israel also was accused of forcing a famine upon the civilians of Gaza. More recently, studies have proven that no famine ever existed, and where there were food shortages, they were caused by Hamas hoarding supplies designated for civilians.

Nonetheless, this year Israel was compelled not only to defend itself against Hamas but also to defend its prosecution of the war before the International Court of Justice (ICJ) in a case brought by the Republic of South Africa accusing Israel of genocide.

We've already gone through the evidence utterly disproving the genocide charge against Israel. The point here is the absurdity that, in the middle of its war against a ruthless and brutal terrorist organization, Israel is called upon to defend itself against charges brought by another nation that is not even affected by the war!

It's not like South Africa was somehow involved in this conflict. And it's not like there weren't other real examples of genocide occurring much closer to South Africa's location such as Darfur. But South Africa chose, nevertheless, to be the single plaintiff in this case.

And there lies the fallacy of the International Court of Justice—the judicial arm of the United Nations. Any member can sue any other member on claims of alleged genocide. In the case of South Africa, it is undisputed that this claim was based on politics, not morality—and more accurately, antisemitism. The Palestinians are very popular within South Africa, and the African National Congress (ANC), dropping fast in the polls in an election season, saw this as a means of regaining favor. After all, South Africa's poverty rate is more than 55 percent.

The ANC lost the election anyway. It seems that even in South Africa, antisemitism is not a powerful enough force to prevail at the ballot box.

Perhaps to highlight its bias, and seemingly as a matter of pride, the South African delegation presenting its case against Israel included Jeremy Corbyn, the former head of the British Labour Party, who was banished from the party as an antisemite. Another leader of the delegation was John Dugard, a longtime UN staffer and critic of Israel.

The United States, Germany, and other Western nations described the charges as baseless, but in the Alice in Wonderland world of the UN, every rogue nation gets a chance to take a shot against Israel. In the end, the ICJ did not find any evidence that Israel had committed genocide, but it has retained jurisdiction over the matter and undoubtedly will issue disturbing rulings in the future that will be rejected by many in Israel and the West.

To put a broader point on this, the United Nations is a cosmic failure in its stated aim of maintaining world peace. And the problems are structural.

The two primary bodies of the United Nations are the General Assembly and the Security Council. The General

Assembly is run on the basis of one nation, one vote among all 193 members. With Israel as a single Jewish state among many hostile neighbors, it never wins. Fortunately, the GA is mostly irrelevant, offering nonbinding recommendations and dealing with appointments and budgetary matters.

The Security Council is where significant issues of war and peace are raised. There are fourteen members of the council, nine of which rotate and five of which—the United States, the UK, France, Russia, and China—are permanent members with veto rights. Israel has never been a member of the Security Council.

Because Russia and China can veto any Security Council resolution, and because they see attacks against Israel as attacks against the Western nations with whom they are adversaries, there has never been a Security Council resolution condemning Hamas, notwithstanding almost two decades of sustained war crimes by Hamas against Israeli civilians.

The United Nations and its agencies, the self-appointed vanguards of international law around the world, thus have structural failings ranging from the impotent to the malign. To make matters even worse, organizations such as UNRWA have now been found to have had members actively assisting in the Hamas massacre.

When I was in office, I remember the fervent efforts of Ambassador Nikki Haley to get just the General Assembly to offer a slap on the wrist to Hamas. She came close but could not get enough votes. That beautiful building on Second Avenue and Forty-Fourth Street in New York City is an ethical cesspool!

The failings of the United Nations are only half of the problem. The other half is the academic—as contrasted with the judicial—approach to Israel's legal entitlement to its biblical homeland. It is subject to a robust but ultimately phony debate that unfortunately has been either mistakenly or intentionally misstated by the United States as a justification to punish Israel.

When World War I came to an end, the defeated Ottoman Empire relinquished its claims to the territory (not the nation, because there was none) of Palestine in favor of the British mandate to achieve a national home for the Jewish people. At that time, Palestine was inhabited by Jews, who had a three-thousand-year-old documented historic connection to the land, and Arabs, many of them nomadic, who were culturally and historically indistinguishable from Palestinians in Jordan and elsewhere.

As we discussed earlier, the United Nations ultimately authorized a Jewish state and an Arab state in the territory that remained of Palestine. Although Israel accepted the plan, the Arab countries bordering Israel and several others rejected the UN's plan and attacked Israel when it declared its independence. Israel won the war; it won numerous additional wars begun by Arab nations, and its borders expanded as it fended off these attacks.

All the territory captured by Israel in the 1967 Six-Day War was subject to a resolution in the UN Security Council—Resolution 242. This resolution is the *only* agreement between all the warring parties (Syria signed on a few years later), and therefore, in contrast to all the other one-sided politically driven noise, this resolution does have some legal effect. Importantly, the Palestinians were not parties to Resolution 242—the territory of Judea and Samaria was represented then by Jordan.

The resolution was heavily negotiated. The demand made of Israel was that it withdraw from "all the territories" it captured in 1967. Israel refused to accept such a blanket withdrawal, agreeing only to withdraw from "territories" in exchange for "peace within secure and recognized boundaries."

The United States played an active role in mediating the negotiations over Resolution 242. Its representatives to that mediation were former Supreme Court Justice Arthur Goldberg, then the U.S. ambassador to the United Nations, and Eugene Rostow, the U.S. undersecretary of state for political affairs at the time. Rostow went on to become the dean of the Yale Law School.

The territory Israel captured during the Six-Day War included the Old City of Jerusalem, the Sinai Peninsula, the Gaza Strip, Judea and Samaria, and the Golan Heights. The principles of Resolution 242 (later Resolution 338 to include Syria) address the disposition of each of these territories.

Sinai was returned to Egypt in the 1979 peace treaty. Israel achieved "peace with secure and recognized boundaries" as part of that treaty in accordance with Resolution 242.

In contrast, the objectives of Resolution 242 were not achievable for Israel were it to withdraw from either Jerusalem or the Golan Heights. Israel formally exercised its sovereignty over Jerusalem almost immediately upon the capture of the eastern part of the city. It exercised its sovereignty over the Golan Heights in 1981. In both cases, the United States under the Trump administration recognized that sovereignty. The United States should have done so decades earlier.

Shortly after President Trump recognized Israeli sovereignty over the Golan Heights, Secretary of State Mike Pompeo and I authored an article in the *Wall Street*

Journal explaining how that recognition was consistent with Resolution 242. Here's what we said:

> Resolution 242 calls on the parties to negotiate a just and lasting peace, one that recognizes the right of all countries, including Israel, to live "within secure and recognized boundaries free from threats or acts of force." It provides that Israel would withdraw from some—but not necessarily all—territory captured in 1967 in keeping with that objective. Some of Israel's former enemies pursued peace in good faith, and Israel has withdrawn from 88% of the territory it captured in 1967—most notably the Sinai Peninsula, pursuant to the 1979 Camp David Accords with Egypt.
>
> Syria is a different story. In word and deed, Damascus has for 52 years rejected the negotiating framework of Resolution 242. It has maintained a state of war with Israel since Israel became independent in 1948. It is a client of Iran and one of the most brutal regimes on earth. By affirming Israel's sovereignty over the Golan Heights, the president has afforded Israel the only secure and recognized boundary that can exist under the circumstances—the objective of Resolution 242.

After October 7 and probably before, the same argument that Secretary Pompeo and I made regarding the Golan Heights could and should be made for Judea and Samaria. Its Palestinian inhabitants wholeheartedly support Hamas, "a client of Iran and one of the most brutal regimes on earth." Hamas will never accept Israel's borders wherever drawn, and its influence will remain even when the war ends (especially if it ends as Biden now demands, with Hamas retaining a claim to power). Resolution 242 entitles Israel to retain all of Judea and

Samaria, just as it does the Golan Heights, to achieve "secure and recognized boundaries."

Moreover, the only nation with a competing claim to Judea and Samaria as of the adoption of Resolution 242 was Jordan, the nation from which it was captured. Jordan has since renounced any claim to the territory in its treaty with Israel in 1994.

In 1991, Dean Rostow wrote the following in the *New Republic*:

> Resolution 242, which as undersecretary of state for political affairs between 1966 and 1969 I helped produce, calls on the parties to make peace. . . . When such a peace is made, Israel is required to withdraw its armed forces "from territories" . . . not from "the" territories nor from "all" territories, but from some of the territories, which included the Sinai Desert, the West Bank, the Golan Heights, East Jerusalem and the Gaza Strip.

Rostow went on to say,

> The British Mandate recognized the right of the Jewish people to "close settlement" in the whole of the mandated territory. It was provided that local conditions might require Great Britain to "postpone" or "withhold" Jewish settlement in what is now Jordan. This was done in 1922. But the Jewish right of settlement in Palestine west of the Jordan River, that is, in Israel, the West Bank [a.k.a. Judea and Samaria], Jerusalem and the Gaza Strip was made unassailable. That right has never been terminated and cannot be terminated except by a recognized peace between Israel and its neighbors.

We could do a much deeper dive into international law as it applies to Judea and Samaria, but the reality is that the law consists of nonbinding opinions by lawyers and courts that suffer from the same infirmities as the politicization of the United Nations that we already discussed.

Most of the opinions adverse to Israel center on Article 49 of the Geneva Convention which prohibits a nation from conquering territory and then moving its population into that territory—something Hitler did as he marched through parts of Europe. The application of this principle to Israel and Judea and Samaria is grotesque for several reasons:

1. Israel was not the aggressor in the Six-Day War. It was defending itself against an attack from Jordan.
2. Only Israel, and not Jordan, had rights in Judea and Samaria—from 1948 until 1967, virtually the entire world agreed that Jordan was occupying the territory illegally.
3. While occupying Judea and Samaria, Jordan prohibited Jews from visiting the holy sites located there—even the Western Wall.
4. When Israel captured Judea and Samaria in 1967, it was repatriating territory that had been promised to it both by God in the Bible and by the San Remo Declaration. It was not an "occupier" of foreign land.
5. Israel never forced any of its population to move to Judea and Samaria. Those who moved did so of their own personal, ideological, and/or theological volition.

There remains today only one relevant agreement—Resolution 242. It doesn't suffer from political manipulation; it is essentially a contract. The Palestinians aren't even parties to that contract, although they occasionally acknowledge its application and then misinterpret it.

According to the United States' "man in the room"— the highly distinguished diplomat and academic who negotiated Resolution 242—Israel's right to settle its citizens in Judea and Samaria is "unassailable." That ought to be the end of the inquiry, at least with respect to the foreign policy of the United States of America. And that was the reason that the Pompeo Doctrine came to be.

Unfortunately, both the Biden administration and the Obama administration have taken a different view, contrary to that taken by U.S. government officials who knew the issue best. They contend that Jewish settlement in Judea and Samaria is illegal. Obama even allowed a Security Council resolution to that effect (Resolution 2334) to pass in the waning days of his administration, inflicting upon Israel a great betrayal. They were wrong and should be ashamed for taking a contradictory and erroneous legal position solely to achieve a political goal—pressuring Israel to surrender its biblical territory.

In the end, however, apart from Resolution 242, international law offers little to resolve the conflict regarding Judea and Samaria. The legal positions differ among the parties, the anti-Israel opinions reek of political bias, and there is no court with jurisdiction to decide and then enforce its decision.

The relevant issues are practical and theological. Practically, the Palestinians cannot form an independent state that will not be a threat to itself and others or a state that will end the cycle of hatred, violence, and poverty. That can only be achieved under Israeli sovereignty with assistance from moderate Sunni nations.

Theologically, no good outcome will be achieved by giving the biblical heartland of the Jewish people to others who do not respect the words of the Bible or the holiness of the land. I should say it even more strongly: God's grant to the Jewish people may not be rescinded.

10
CAN THERE BE A TWO-STATE SOLUTION?

The answer to the question is "NO!" And I know this because we tried. In the Trump administration we spent years crafting a Vision for Peace that we hoped might be acceptable to Israelis and Palestinians alike.

It was called a "realistic" two-state solution. The Palestinians would have been granted a "state" in a literal sense, but that state would not have had many attributes of statehood. Israel would have controlled the state's airspace, its electromagnetic spectrum, and its borders. Israel also would have maintained the right of entry into this state in pursuit of terrorists or to thwart planned but not yet committed terror attacks.

The proposed borders of this Palestinian "state" would have included all of Areas A and B and about half of Area C within Judea and Samaria. The Jewish settlements all would have been incorporated into Israel, and Palestinian communities that were not contiguous with each other would be connected through bridges and tunnels.

This was the first time in history that Israel had ever agreed to a map within which it would live side by side with Palestinians.

The Vision for Peace, however, did not guarantee that the Palestinians would actually receive this modified "state." There were targets that needed to be achieved first, including

- The establishment of a Palestinian constitution or similar governing document providing for freedom of the press, freedom of religion for minorities, fair elections, uniform and fair enforcement of law and contractual rights, due process of law, and an independent judiciary.
- The establishment of transparent, independent, and credit-worthy financial institutions capable of engaging in international market transactions with appropriate governance to prevent corruption.
- The ending of all "pay for slay" programs and educational incitement of hatred against Jews.

I struggled with the plan because of its potential nominal creation of a Palestinian state, even with all the practical limitations on statehood. I received many objections as well from the observant Christian and Jewish communities. Even though this plan offered far more land within Judea and Samaria than ever before to the State of Israel—incorporating every Jewish settlement into Israel—the idea of a state for Palestinians, no matter how that grant was spun, was anathema to their religious beliefs. In retrospect, they were right. The plan would have left places like Joseph's Tomb and Mount Ebal, the home of the Tomb of Joshua, under Palestinian autonomy, and it would have created a precedent for statehood that the Palestinians would have manipulated with more left-wing governments.

I did think the Vision for Peace made sense as a template for further negotiations if Israel ever had its back to the wall in its dealings with a Democratic administration. Although it had its deficiencies, this was a far better starting point for Israel than anything proposed by Biden, Obama, Clinton, or Bush. The plan also created an opening for moderate Sunni nations like the United Arab Emirates to get closer to Israel—it led to the Abraham Accords.

But the bottom line is that the Vision for Peace was pilloried by Mahmoud Abbas. Here was a detailed offer from the United States and Israel for specific territory with enormous financial backing. And yet Mahmoud Abbas, in the face of arguably the best deal the Palestinians have ever been offered in terms of the specifics and quality of life, went to the Security Council, ripped up the document, and shouted various and sundry curses in Arabic at the sponsors.

The lesson to be learned here is twofold. First, the Palestinian leadership is far more interested in the negative than the positive. They don't covet advances that will make their people safer, healthier, or more prosperous. They desire concrete steps that will damage Israel and ultimately lead to its destruction. In particular, they seek international delegitimization of Israel's connection to its biblical heritage as an essential means of destroying the Jewish state.

Second, the notion of a peace-loving Palestinian state living side by side with Israel is a cruel fallacy. The Vision for Peace had a long list of preconditions for the Palestinians to become stateworthy. The list demonstrates vividly just how far away they are from that goal. And the reality is that the Palestinian leadership has no interest in going down that path. Remember that not a single Muslim nation in the Middle East is a democracy. Mahmoud Abbas has no interest in his state being the first one.

And then, of course, comes October 7 as the exclamation point on this issue. A vicious attack, indescribable in its barbarity, viewed with pride and regaled in glory by more than four-fifths of Palestinians in Judea and Samaria. The notion that such feelings of hatred should be rewarded with an independent state is nothing less than grotesque.

And yet that is exactly what the Biden administration has been pushing both before and after October 7. It is an administration infused with Israel bashers, including

- Hady Amr, the special envoy to the Palestinians, a newly created position in the Biden administration, who has said he was "inspired" by the violent Intifada against Israel and supports the Boycott, Divestment, and Sanctions (BDS) movement.
- Reema Dodin, the deputy director of the White House Office of Legislative Affairs who had excused Palestinian suicide bombings.
- Maher Bitar, the director of defense policy at the National Security Council, once a leader of Students for Justice in Palestine, a Marxist sponsor of anti-Israel demonstrations who was reported to have organized an anti-Israel conference and ran a session on how to demonize Israel.
- Robert Malley, the United States' lead Iran negotiator who led Obama's team in negotiating the disastrous Joint Comprehensive Plan of Action (JCPOA) and who is now on suspension for reported security

violations. He was also reported to be Yasser Arafat's godson!

- Rabbi Sharon Kleinbaum, an appointee to the U.S. Committee on International Religious Freedom who, just one day after the October 7 massacre, shamelessly implied (with no evidence whatsoever) that the Israeli government had permitted progressive Jews in the south to be slaughtered while improperly protecting "settlers" in Judea and Samaria.

The list goes on. And it points to an important and unfortunate fact: even when political leaders within the Democratic Party spout platitudes about protecting Israel, the people who run the critical agencies and advise the leaders mostly come from the breeding pools of woke academia and far-left institutions. They have a discernible anti-Israel bias.

Oddly, while about 80 percent of Americans are more sympathetic to Israel than the Palestinians, the national divide between Republicans and Democrats is about fifty-fifty. And even if a majority of the Democrats support Israel (likely a faulty assumption), when a Democratic candidate becomes president, he or she will draw a staff of Middle East policy "experts" from the usual places that are decidedly anti-Israel. This leaves Israel in a precarious position of having a fifty-fifty chance every four years that there will be a hostile U.S. president who will attempt to force upon it a two-state solution.

It happened with Clinton, with Obama, and now with Biden. And it will happen again as long as there is intellectual and diplomatic vitality to the two-state solution. We must end both.

The two-state solution agenda also goes well beyond just asking Israel to cede its biblical heartland in exchange for a naked and unreliable promise to end violent hostilities. Accompanying this particular initiative is a package of policies that endanger Israel's very existence.

Two-staters mostly support granting Iran relief from sanctions enforcement, resulting in a steady stream of terrorist training and funding for all the bad actors in the Middle East, from the Houthis to Hezbollah to Hamas to Islamic Jihad and others. They think—all evidence to the contrary—that this will cause Iran to moderate its malign behavior.

Two-staters also wrongfully consider Israelis living within Judea and Samaria to be breaking international law. In Biden's case, he has gone so far as to inject himself into Israel's internal law enforcement process and sanction Jewish residents who the United States believes have been violent toward Palestinians. Never mind the fact that Palestinian violence against Israelis is many multiples of the reverse—a reality I came to observe personally in my four years as ambassador. Biden has never sanctioned a Palestinian for misconduct of this nature.

Two-staters also embrace the United Nations as an institution capable of resolving issues in the Middle East. The Obama administration permitted passage of a Security Council resolution that deemed all of Judea and Samaria and East Jerusalem (even the Western Wall) to be illegally occupied territory. Biden permitted passage of a Security Council resolution demanding a ceasefire by Israel in its current war against Hamas without requiring the release of the hostages as a precondition and without condemning Hamas. Both administrations also fund UNRWA and participate as members in the United Nations Human Rights Council, an organization led by rogue and/or autocratic nations like Iran and China. At every meeting, there is only one nation that permanently is on the agenda for condemnation for human rights violations—Israel.

As I have said many times, the two-state solution is a "final solution" (Hitler's term for exterminating the Jews) for the State of Israel and the Jewish people. We cannot let this advance.

The two-state solution needs to enter the dustbin of history. On April 30, 2024, President Trump, in an interview with *Time*, said the following: "Most people thought it was going to be a two-state solution. I'm not sure a two-state solution anymore is gonna work."

After President Trump made those comments, I authored a letter of thanks on behalf of the "Keep God's Land" coalition—a group of faith leaders who encourage Israeli sovereignty over Judea and Samaria. Within two days, more than four hundred faith leaders cosigned the letter.

President Trump was absolutely right, and he should know. We spent thousands of hours from 2017 to 2021 listening to competing points of view on the Israeli-Palestinian conflict. We spoke with everyone who had a dog in the hunt. And we heard the despicable language and witnessed the barbaric violence of the Palestinians condoned, and often encouraged, by their leaders.

Since the October 7 massacre, college campuses across the country have become increasingly more violent with throngs of protestors—many of whom are not students—siding with Hamas over Israel. These Jew-haters are not crying out for peace, for a fair settlement between the parties, or for a return of the suffering hostages. Not a single sign calls for a two-state solution.

Those siding with Hamas want "Palestine from the River to the Sea"—that is, they want to eliminate Israel. And they want "only one solution, Intifada revolution"—that is, to destroy Israel through violence.

We should listen to what they say and make sure that they never achieve their goals. Whether or not there are Palestinians willing to live side by side with Israel in peace is not the issue. Even if the answer is yes, there are far too few. God seems to be asking us over and over again, "What more do you need to be convinced not to give away the land that I have given to the Jewish people?" By now, we should all be convinced.

11

MAY ONE NEGOTIATE LAND FOR PEACE UNDER JEWISH LAW?

The notion of "land for peace" has been the foundation stone of almost all proposed resolutions of the Israeli-Palestinian conflict. It is a concept that was conditionally agreed to by the State of Israel when it signed off on Resolution 242. But does it comport with Jewish Law?

I am not a rabbi or a serious student of Jewish Law. If this were a tough question, I would defer to others who were more qualified. But the law here is straightforward, and its application to the facts is abundantly clear.

As we have discussed, there is no prohibition on Israel negotiating and agreeing to peace with the Palestinians in the absence of a surrender of territory. But what if peace requires such a surrender?

The Bible certainly speaks about the affirmative obligation of Jews to settle in Israel. For example, in the book of Numbers 33:53, God states, "And you shall take possession of the land and settle in it, for I have assigned the land to you to possess."

Not all biblical scholars have included the obligation to settle the land of Israel among the 613 commandments by God to the Jewish people. But all would agree that, once settled, the defense of the land of Israel against its enemies is an "obligatory war" and hence a commandment.

In Jewish Law, however, there is an overriding concept called "Pikuach Nefesh"—a life-or-death emergency. Under those circumstances, almost all commandments are suspended, and the entire focus must be the saving of the affected lives. One may desecrate the Sabbath (by, for example, driving in a car) or permit one in poor health to eat on Yom Kippur if needed to save a life.

One of the most authoritative rulings on whether an agreement of land for peace violates Jewish Law was issued by Rabbi Ovadia Yosef of blessed memory, one of the most respected scholars of the modern State of Israel and once Israel's Chief Sephardic Rabbi. His ruling was sought on the eve of the Oslo Accords. The issue was whether making peace averted a "Pikuach Nefesh." This was his initial ruling:

> If the heads and commanders of the army, together with the government, state that saving of life is involved; that if areas of Israel are not given back, the danger exists of immediate war on the part of our Arab neighbors; And if the areas are returned to them, the danger of war will be averted; and that there is a chance of permanent peace; then it seems that according to all opinions it is permitted to return areas of Israel in order to achieve this aim, since nothing is more important than the saving of life.

Less than nine years later, Rabbi Yosef realized that he had been sold a bill of goods by the politicians who sought his advice. Apparently frustrated by how his words had been manipulated, he clarified that his prior view presumed a certainty of real peace, not the hypothetical or aspirational peace that supported Oslo. In 2003, he said the following:

> My dear brothers of Israel, residents of Judea and Samaria:
>
> It is my intention to make clear my position concerning Judea and Samaria. I have explained more than once my Halachic [Jewish Law] ruling, that giving up land for peace has no validity in light of the current situation.
>
> I had intended only and purely authentic peace, one in which Jerusalem and its surroundings will be secure in peace and quiet. But now, our eyes see that surrendering our holy land causes a danger to life.
>
> This is not the peace for which we prayed. Therefore, the Oslo Accords are null and void.

One of the greatest Rabbinic authorities of the twentieth century was the Lubavitcher Rebbe, Rabbi Menachem Mendel Schneerson, referred to by thousands as the "Rebbe." Today, more than five thousand ordained rabbis bring the Rebbe's message to the four corners of the earth. One would be hard-pressed to visit a city today that lacks a "Chabad House," the house of worship and study founded by the Rebbe.

Like Rabbi Yosef, the Rebbe (and virtually all others) agreed that the only lawful means to surrender land for peace was if it averted a Pikuach Nefesh. And he further acknowledged that this was a military decision rather than one that could be assessed by clergy. But he was highly skeptical, to the point of being dismissive, of military arguments that were speculative or that bled into social, economic, or political considerations.

The Rebbe, in a letter to the chief rabbi of the United Kingdom, initially made it clear: "I am completely and unequivocally opposed to the surrender of any of the liberated areas currently under negotiation, such as Yehuda and Shomron [Judea and Samaria], the Golan, etc."

In keeping with other authorities, he agreed that the only means by which his view could be changed was in the event of a Pikuach Nefesh. But he rejected prognostications of future harm—there needed to be an immediate and concrete threat to life that would be averted by the agreement:

> To argue that the fate of the country and the lives of the people depend also on factors beyond the competence of military experts, and that if political and economic factors will be ignored, it would lead to Pikuach Nefesh later on, does not affect the immediate decision in relation to the return of territories. All the more so since it is certain that returning further territories will immediately weaken security, and would be an irreversible act, whereas the political and economic climate is unpredictable.

The architecture of Jewish Law begins with 613 commandments, of which 248 require an affirmative action and 365 proscribe actions considered sinful. Not all scholars agree on the precise identity of every commandment; many but not all consider the settlement of the land of Israel to be one of them.

Above that layer of commandments sits an overriding exception: Pikuach Nefesh, the performance of commandments can be deferred or even negated if urgently necessary to save a life.

And above that exception lies an exception to the exception: even to save a life, one may not engage in any of these three prohibitions: murder, worshipping false gods, and adultery.

Within this architecture—and as explicated by Rabbi Yosef, Rabbi Schneerson, and many others—the burden to justify land for peace is exceptionally high. It would require, literally, a military opinion that surrender will result in an immediate saving of human life. Longer-term political or economic benefits of such surrender are of no relevance to the determination.

Such a determination would also require a "real world" evaluation of the present circumstances along with historical evidence. For example, one would need to look at the Gaza experience and undoubtedly conclude that, in that case, the surrender of territory was disastrous and cost many lives. Indeed, no lives were saved.

In the aftermath of October 7, now with certainty that surrendering land brings only violence and that such violence is endorsed by at least four of every five Palestinians, it is inconceivable that surrendering tangible territory for a naked and likely false promise of peace could satisfy the requirements of Jewish Law. Not being a rabbi, I cannot say this with the authoritative certainty that such a pedigree would provide. But the law does seem clear.

12

HOW TO LOVE THE STRANGER

Up to this point, some readers may have developed some strong negative feelings toward the Palestinians, others some strong negative feelings toward me. While I don't want to get between anyone and their feelings, my message has not been all that controversial from a historical perspective: the Palestinian leadership has always been corrupt, it embraces violent uprisings against Jews as a means of political advancement, it seeks to destroy Israel, and it has no track record or political platform of non-threatening self-governance.

But what about individual Palestinians? Surely there are those who would live in peace with their Jewish cousins. What should be done with them?

The Bible gives us enormous guidance on this issue, both on an individualized basis and on a collective basis.

In terms of Palestinian individuals, the Torah commands the Jew to love and protect the stranger. That sounds like a good place to start. The question is, who is "the stranger?"

Most biblical commentaries refer to the stranger as a convert to Judaism. The best source for that is Numbers 15:16: "One Torah and one law shall apply to you and to the stranger who dwells in your midst." If a single Torah applies to the stranger, plainly we are speaking about a stranger who has accepted the Torah—a convert. Indeed, to this day, the Hebrew word for convert—*Ger*—is the same as the word for stranger contained in the biblical text.

But then there's the language of Deuteronomy 10:19: "And you shall love the stranger because you were strangers in the land of Egypt." In this context, the stranger should not mean a convert, since Jews in Egypt were not converts. Here, although I am no biblical scholar, one can argue that the stranger means someone alone or unfamiliar with his surroundings.

Some theologians read from this a biblical mandate for Israel to love Palestinians as "strangers." That is quite a leap of reasoning insofar as Palestinians, while the minority population in Israel, hardly qualify as being a minority in the region or unfamiliar with their surroundings. But there still is more biblical authority that applies.

Leviticus 19:33–34 offers an important distinction between being a citizen and being a "stranger": "When a stranger resides with you in your land you shall not wrong him. The stranger who resides with you shall be to you as if he was one of your citizens; you shall love him as you love yourselves because you were strangers in the land of Egypt, I am the Lord your God."

Here, the Bible plainly recognizes that, in the land of Israel, there are Jews who are "citizens" and there are "strangers" who "reside with you in your land." The Jews are not commanded to make the strangers citizens of Israel. But they are commanded, very clearly, to love them and not to wrong them.

The status of such a stranger is codified, first in the Bible and then in Rabbinic law. The phrase in Hebrew is *Ger Toshav*, a resident alien—not unlike the holder of a "Green Card" in the United States. Leviticus 25:35 states, "If your brother becomes poor and cannot maintain himself with you, you shall support him as though he were a resident alien, and he shall live with you."

The Bible thus recognizes a residency status, short of citizenship, that entitles the resident to live within the land of Israel free of persecution or discrimination.

During the Talmudic period it was determined that for Gentiles to achieve the rights of a resident alien in Israel, they were required to take upon themselves the commitment to observe the seven Noahide Laws (the laws observed by the sons of Noah). They are as follows:

1. Not to worship idols
2. Not to curse God
3. Not to commit murder
4. Not to commit adultery
5. Not to steal
6. Not to eat a limb from a living animal
7. To establish courts of justice

These are hardly burdensome obligations. In fact, many of them today would likely be necessary requirements of many civilized countries before they accept an immigrant. Under Jewish Law, permanent residency, but not citizenship, was available to those willing to accept these minimal requirements.

On an individual basis, the Bible thus encourages us to live respectfully among non-Jewish residents and commands us to treat them with respect. But what about nations that are committed to Israel's destruction? The Bible speaks to that as well.

The analysis begins with Genesis chapter 15 and God's "covenant of the parts" to Abraham. God foretells that Abraham's descendants will be slaves in a foreign country. They will not return to the future land of Israel (then the land of Canaan) for some time: "The fourth generation will return because the sin of the Amorites will not have been complete until then" (verse 16).

God is not simply replacing the Jewish nation with the Amorites and the other six nations who inhabited the land of Canaan. He would not displace them until their collective sins were such that they deserved to be defeated and dispersed. Indeed, the seven nations—the Canaanites, the Hittites, the Amorites, the Perizzites, the Jebusites, the Girgashites, and the Hivites (collectively, the Seven Nations of Canaan)—were known to be so immoral that both Abraham and Isaac demanded that their sons not take wives from that region. The Bible describes Canaanite practices as including the worship of demonic idols, prohibited sexual acts, and even the sacrifice of children.

There is not much ambiguity in God's commandment to destroy the Seven Nations of Canaan. This is what he instructs in Deuteronomy 7:1–6:

> The Lord your God will bring you into the Land. You are going to enter it and take it as your own. He'll drive out many nations to make room for you. He'll drive out the Hittites, Girgashites, Amorites, Canaanites, Perizzites, Hivites and Jebusites. Those seven nations are larger and stronger than you are. The Lord your God will hand them over to you. You will win the battle over them. You must completely destroy them. Don't

make a peace treaty with them. Don't show them any mercy. Don't marry any of their people. Don't give your daughters to their sons. And don't take their daughters for their sons. . . . So here is what you must do to those people. Break down their altars. Smash their sacred stones. Cut down the poles they use to worship the female god named Asherah. Burn the statues of their gods in the fire. You are a holy nation.

Fortunately, there is no theological application of these laws to the Palestinians insofar as the Palestinians are not one of the Seven Nations of Canaan. Most say that Arabs didn't arrive in Israel until 1,500 years later. It is a lesson, however, about the limits of mercy, a brake on the overriding concept of kindness and fairness to the stranger.

The point is best illustrated by the story of King Saul, the first king of Israel. He was commanded by God to vanquish the Amalekite nation, including its king, Agag. Saul led an army to defeat the Amalekites but left Agag alive. Samuel the prophet was forced to execute Agag by himself and God stripped Saul of his kingship. According to legend, during the period when Agag remained alive, he was able to procreate and create a lineage that included Haman, the evil prince of the Purim story who tried to destroy the Jewish nation.

There is the well-known saying that being merciful to the evil brings evil upon the merciful. That is the lesson of Saul and Agag, and that lesson needs to be internalized within the context of Israel's war against Hamas. The war must be won; Hamas must be destroyed. Civilians should be spared, but not at the expense of victory.

Importantly, the Bible does not direct the Israelite nation to disdain from living in peace with nations other than the Seven Nations of Canaan, and even then, when Joshua made a treaty with the Gibeonites (part of the Hivites) under false pretenses, he kept his covenant of peace even though he had been defrauded. Indeed, there is an ancient nation—the Kenites—who lived in harmony with the Jewish nation from the time of the exodus from Egypt. To this day, the descendants of Jews and Kenites continue to live in peace within the State of Israel.

The Kenites are first mentioned in Genesis 15:18 as one of the nations that the people of Israel will one day conquer upon their return to the land of Israel. But it didn't work out that way. The Kenites embraced the Israelites and developed an ancient bond that remains.

The relationship between the Israelites and the Kenites was created when Moses fled Egypt after Pharaoh discovered that he was a Hebrew. Moses ultimately found shelter with the Kenite tribe living in the land of Midian. The head of the tribe was named Jethro, who became Moses's father-in-law when Moses married his daughter, Tzipporah. Moses lived with the Kenites for several years.

Moses then returned to Egypt to rescue his enslaved people and began the trek to Canaan after the exodus. Along the way, Moses rejoined Jethro, and the Kenite tribe traveled with the Israelites to the Promised Land.

So aligned were the Israelites with the Kenites that Balaam—the pagan prophet hired by Balak, the king of Moab, to curse Israel—looked out at the Israelite nation and the Kenite tribe and blessed both of them, proclaiming as to the Kenites, "Your dwelling place is secure and your nest is set in rock" (Numbers 24:21).

In the days of the biblical judges, the Israelite prophetess Deborah was at war with an enemy named Sisrah. A Kenite named Hever came to her aid. His wife, Yael, lured

Sisrah into her tent, gave him a drink that caused him to sleep, and killed him, thereby ending the war. Yael is considered one of the great heroes in the Bible—so much so that Ivanka Trump took Yael as her Hebrew name!

We can fast-forward to modern times and observe something incredible: Jethro, the head of the ancient Kenite tribe, is also the principal prophet of the Druze faith. And Israel has no more loyal minority within its borders than the Druze.

There are about 150,000 Druze living in Israel. They are non-Muslim and Arabic-speaking and support the State of Israel and the Zionist cause. Druze serve in the Israel Defense Forces (IDF), many having attained high ranks. Druze also have attained significant positions in Israeli commerce, science, academia, and finance. The Jewish majority in Israel has great appreciation and affection for the Druze minority.

The Bible thus has many important lessons regarding how the State of Israel can and should deal with its minorities that remain highly relevant today.

The obligation to "love the stranger" can fairly be interpreted to mean that Israel must not afflict its minorities and should provide in a reasonable manner for their welfare. The notion of a "resident alien" means that individuals inhabiting the land who agree to live in peace with Israel should be entitled to live on their land and protected against eviction or other harm. And the lesson of the Kenites is that entire non-Jewish ethnic populations can live side by side in peace within the single Jewish state.

The Palestinians accuse Israel of engaging in some sort of religious conspiracy to suppress their human rights. They could not be more wrong. The architecture of biblical settlement within the land of Israel is replete with admonitions that minorities living in peace with their neighbors must be protected. The Bible also mandates that those refusing to live in peace with Israel must be defeated—that's not a religious conspiracy; it's the only modality for Jewish survival!

This biblical wisdom rings just as true today as three thousand years ago. It is the divine teachings of the past and the divine path to the future.

13
THE TEMPLATE FOR COEXISTENCE

The flawed thesis of the two-state solution is that Jews and Arabs must live apart, that their differences are so irreconcilable that nothing short of complete separation will resolve their conflict. The thesis is, of course, self-contradictory insofar as the proposed plan would create a fully separate—*Judenrein*—Palestinian state, while Israel would remain open to all ethnicities.

But in addition to being hypocritical, the plan is demonstrably wrong. It is founded on the misguided views of the political class—the elites of the United States and the EU and the corrupt among the Palestinians—who see the conflict as ideological, territorial, and highly profitable to continue. They have no relationship with working people or any understanding of their priorities and thus have lost all popular support from within their constituencies.

The two-state crowd ignores the two indisputable realities staring them in the face: first, that the already existing Palestinian state in Jordan is an autocratic failure, offering neither freedom nor prosperity to its residents. Second, the Palestinians living in Israel—also known as Arab Israeli citizens, have the best standard of living in the Middle East.

Let's not forget that the difference in status between Israeli Arabs and Palestinians is based on the happenstance of where they were located when the Armistice Line (the Green Line) of 1949 was drawn up. Those on the west side of that line hit the jackpot and became Israelis, those to the east were stuck in Jordan until 1967 and now live in unresolved circumstances.

So what's a better option? Creating a second Palestinian state likely to fail and be overrun by terrorists or absorbing Judea and Samaria into Israel? While the answer should be obvious, we can put a finer point on this by looking more deeply into the lives of Israeli Arabs.

Ishmael Khaldi is an Arab citizen of Israel. He was born in a village close to Haifa and lived in a Bedouin tent until the age of eight. He graduated with a bachelor's degree from the University of Haifa, earned a master's degree in political science from Tel Aviv University, served in the IDF, and got a job in the Ministry of Foreign Affairs as the vice consul in San Francisco. In August 2009, he was appointed as policy advisor to Israel's right-wing minister of foreign affairs, Avigdor Lieberman, who Khaldi describes as "one of the most realistic, of course, but honest and direct politicians in Israel."

Khaldi is deeply committed to advancing the rights of Israel's Bedouin community. He recognizes that there remains work to do in creating a fully equal environment for Israel's Arab minority. Nonetheless, here is how he describes the situation:

I am a proud Israeli—along with many other non-Jewish Israelis such as Druze, Bahai, Bedouin, Christians, and Muslims, who live in one of the most culturally diversified societies and the only true democracy in the Middle East. Like America, Israeli society is far from perfect, but let us deal honestly. By any yardstick you choose—educational opportunity, economic development, women and gay's rights, freedom of speech and assembly, legislative representation—Israel's minorities fare better than any other country in the Middle East.

Israel, of course, answers to a higher authority than a calling to be better than repressive Muslim dictatorships. It is obligated, and it accepts the obligation, to respect the sanctity of every human life. I won't sugarcoat this issue and tell you that there is no discrimination in Israel. There is, just like everywhere that there is a minority population that is ethnically or culturally different. But Israel prides itself in the respect it gives its minorities, and the results speak for themselves.

My favorite data point is Arab enrollment within Israel's universities. Many are world-class institutions and offer real opportunities to their graduates to advance and prosper in technology, life sciences, law, and engineering. Recognizing that Arabs constitute about 20 percent of Israel's population, here are the percentages of Arabs enrolled at Israel's top academic institutions:

Hebrew University in Jerusalem: 17 percent (up from 7 percent in 2004)
Haifa University: 41 percent
Tel Aviv University: 16 percent (30 percent in Schools of Architecture and Management)

The Technion: 22 percent (up 200 percent since 2004,
up 350 percent as to Arab women since 2004)

With such a large participation in Israel's elite universities, it is no wonder that the Arab standard of living in Israel is so high.

Of particular relevance are the statistics of Christian Arabs living as citizens of Israel. Their success demonstrates conclusively that the opportunities for advancement in Israeli society are not dependent on being part of the Jewish majority.

Christian Arabs constitute only 2 percent of the Israeli population, yet they provide 17 percent of the university students. A 2010 survey found them to be the most educated of any ethnic group, including Jews. Christian Arabs also represent the highest percentage of Israeli ethnic groups attending medical school.

During my term as ambassador, Israel was experiencing an economic boom derived from its advancements in technology. I was interested in learning if this growth extended to the Arab community, and I was directed to Nazareth, Israel's largest city. What I found there amazed me.

In that sleepy town, where Jesus was raised, there sits a technology center that houses start-ups and more mature businesses engaged in cutting-edge inventions. Because the long distance between Nazareth and the capital markets of Tel Aviv was disadvantageous to these Arab entrepreneurs, I brought many of the venture capitalists and financiers up to Nazareth for a "shark tank" engagement, trying to find matches between money and ideas. The results were incredible. The future for the Arab business community is bright.

Israeli Arabs do feel a certain identity with their counterparts across the Green Line. Some support a Palestinian state, but almost none want to be part of that state. Not surprisingly, they want to remain citizens of Israel.

This is not just conjecture; the issue came up twice, first in 2006 and again in connection with the Trump Vision for Peace.

In Northern Central Israel, there are several Muslim villages referred to collectively as the "Triangle." The largest of the villages, with a population of about sixty thousand, is Umm el-Fahm. In 2006, Avigdor Lieberman, then the deputy prime minister of Israel, suggested that the Green Line be redrawn such that the villages within the Triangle, all of which were straddling the Green Line, would all be east of the Green Line and hence part of the Palestinian state that was under negotiation at the time.

Needless to say, that did not go over well with the residents of these Muslim villages. A poll was taken in Umm el-Fahm regarding which side they preferred. The results were conclusive: 83 percent preferred to live under the jurisdiction of Israel while only 11 percent preferred to join a Palestinian state.

In 2020, we proposed the same redrawing of the Green Line, primarily to explore if the sentiment among Israeli Arabs had changed. It had not. When word got out that this proposal was resurfacing, the outcry from Israeli Arabs and Jews alike was overwhelmingly negative. In the aftermath of that response, we confirmed that we would follow the popular will and the Triangle villages would remain part of Israel under our plan.

Israeli Arabs generally are happy with their nation of citizenship. From polling done in 2006, 63 percent accept Israel as a state of the Jewish people, 77 percent say Israel is a better place to live than other countries about which they are aware, and 59 percent of Israeli Arabs fall into the range from "somewhat patriotic" to "very patriotic"

In 2007 it was reported that Arabs have a home ownership rate of 93 percent versus 70 percent for the Jewish community.

It's not entirely idyllic, however, for Israeli Arabs, and the reason is readily discernible—refusal to serve in the Israeli army. The two poorest segments within Israeli society are Arab Muslims and ultra-Orthodox Jews. The one thing they have in common is their refusal of army service.

The IDF is Israel's melting pot. Military service is mandatory for most citizens, and the army draws eighteen-year-old men and women from all walks of life and all socioeconomic, religious, and cultural backgrounds and trains them toward the common defense of the nation. The army builds resilience, character, and unity among people from across the nation. The reserve system, which requires every soldier to return for a month of service every year even after completing army duty, continuously reinforces the unity and common values of the mission.

No one goes for a job interview in Israel without being asked about their military background. Upward mobility depends on many factors, but a distinguished military career ranks among the most important.

Failure to serve in the military thus creates a distinct disadvantage that translates into diminished earning capacity. We see this clear as day with the two communities that reject army service. Failure to serve also results in much lower government benefits (for both Arabs and the ultra-Orthodox).

In the ultra-Orthodox world (called the Haredi community), this is beginning to change. Israel offers Haredi men the opportunity for community service as a substitute for the army. Some are signing up, and others are joining the military, but not yet in sufficient numbers. With the Supreme Court having mandated service, the Haredi community is likely, certainly over time, to be more participatory in the defense of Israel.

But the government has largely left the Arab citizenry alone. There is no mandatory service on the theory that because most of Israel's battles are against other Arabs, one can't reasonably expect Israel Arabs to participate. And while offered a community service opportunity, with those serving being assigned to work within their local villages, few Arabs have accepted the offer.

The Arab citizens of Israel are protected by the same Basic Laws that protect Jewish citizens. The difference is that the laws impose no civic duty upon Arabs. In hindsight, that probably was a mistake.

Arabs have suffered from the curse of low expectations. Israel has not asked them to serve their country, and they haven't. While this originates from a place of good faith, more should be asked of the Arab community, and more should be given in return when the Arab communities step up and deliver.

Israel has permitted many Arab communities to control their educational curriculum as well, much to their detriment. I recall vividly a visit with Jerusalem mayor Moshe Leon to a new school opened in East Jerusalem. The students were entirely Arab, but the curriculum was set to conform with Israeli educational standards. Most of the parents at the school were reluctant to appear with me in the media, but many said to me privately that the school was a game changer. They were ecstatic that their kids were getting the type of education needed to succeed in the modern world.

For this reason and many others, the Arabs in East Jerusalem are perhaps the least interested in a Palestinian state with East Jerusalem as its capital. Most of these residents derive their livelihood from working in West Jerusalem, and a division of the city would bring them great adversity.

The curse of low expectations also applies to the Arab members of the Israeli Knesset. So as not to embarrass them, no member of the Knesset is required to give an oath of loyalty to the State of Israel. In contrast, from left-wing socialists to right-wing capitalists, every member of the U.S. Congress (along with the president and other senior members of the executive branch) must swear allegiance "to support and defend the Constitution of the United States against all enemies, foreign and domestic."

The notion that Arab citizens duly elected to Israel's parliament need not express their loyalty to the state, the best interests of which they were chosen to advance, puts in high relief the duality of the Arab Israeli experience: they are proud to be Israeli and would rather live in Israel than anywhere else, but they prefer not to enter the political, diplomatic, and military fray between Israel and the Arab states or territories.

And that takes us to the issue of Arab suffrage. How important is it? This is not a suggestion that Arab citizens of Israel should be deprived of the right to vote—that should never be removed. But the Arab voting patterns and their results do provide a window into the effects of Jewish sovereignty over Judea and Samaria with the Arab residents there being treated in the manner of Puerto Rico.

Arab voting in Israel simply is not that meaningful. In a parliamentary government, it is the majority coalition (constituting at least 61 members of the 120-seat Knesset) that controls the governing agenda. The minority has essentially no power. Over the past fifty years, only one Arab party—the Islamist United Arab List under the leadership of Mansour Abbas—has ever joined the coalition, which only lasted for about a year. Abbas (no relation to Mahmoud Abbas) indicated that he would use his influence in the coalition to bring more government resources to the Arab community and not to influence diplomatic affairs.

The takeaway here is that Israeli Arabs largely see their country as a Jewish state in which they lead a satisfactory life. There is no desire to change that, and their perspective on governance is largely focused on local issues. In asserting its sovereignty over Judea and Samaria, Israel would be assuming responsibility for an incremental 20 percent of its population. It is a heavy lift that will require economic assistance from the United States and the Gulf. But the economic burden can be managed. What cannot be absorbed is the demographic risk that the Jewish people lose their right of self-determination in the Holy Land.

The template of Arab Israelis portends a brighter future for Palestinians in Judea and Samaria as well. And it is demonstrably achievable. Palestinians should participate in local governance and there should be "no taxation without representation." But there is both legal and political precedent to limit Palestinian voting to local matters and not to any matter that could alter the character or security of the one Jewish state.

The path to this outcome might be long and arduous. But the qualitative and quantitative attributes of the Arab citizenry within the State of Israel establish a means by which Palestinians in Judea and Samaria can flourish under Israeli sovereignty.

14

"SETTLER VIOLENCE": THE RED HERRING FROM THE FAR LEFT

In the world of news, some stories are referred to as "dog bites man" and others as "man bites dog." The former rarely makes news because it is ordinary and repetitive. The latter, an unusual or surprising occurrence, is what hits the front page.

Palestinian violence against Israeli Jews is a classic "dog bites man" story. It has happened repeatedly, brutally, and tragically since long before Israel was in control of Judea and Samaria—even long before Israel was a state.

Today Palestinian terrorism barely makes the news unless it rises to the level of October 7. The news of a couple driving in Judea and Samaria who are pelted by rocks and thereby veer into a ravine to their death is barely worth a mention in almost all non-Israeli press. But unfortunately, this violence, along with shootings and stabbings of Jewish civilians in Judea and Samaria, happens far too frequently. Israel's Ministry of Foreign Affairs reports extensively on these attacks in its publication titled "Wave of Terror 2015–2023." Never are these barbaric acts condemned by Mahmoud Abbas or other representatives of the Palestinian Authority.

But when a Jewish resident of Judea and Samaria acts out against a Palestinian resident, the *New York Times* reserves space on the front page, and the U.S. State Department rushes to issue a condemnation. To be sure, when a Jew acts violently against a Palestinian other than in self-defense, the act is condemnable, and the aggressor must be prosecuted. And that is exactly what Israel does when that happens!

But violence by Jews just doesn't happen that often. It is the "man bites dog" story. Nonetheless, that is exactly the story that the left-wing media amplifies, such that it now has become the main narrative within the region. It sells newspapers and it plays into the antisemitic wave that is plaguing Jews across the globe.

We all know instinctively who is more at fault. We have all seen and heard Palestinian terrorists call for the elimination of the Jewish people and the destruction of Israel. And we have seen the pictures and videos of all the bloodletting and human carnage for which they are proudly responsible. And we also know that the Palestinian Authority provides rich financial rewards for this heinous behavior.

In contrast, we also have seen and heard the voices of the Israeli right. Many may disagree with their views, many may see them as insensitive to Palestinian suffering, but no one thinks they are inciting Jews to inflict physical harm upon their Palestinian neighbors.

I know this personally because I have visited many Jewish cities and villages in Judea and Samaria. I have yet to hear a single leader of those communities call for violence against or eviction of his Palestinian neighbors. I have not seen a single member of any community who wants anything more than to live in peace within his community.

As a general matter, Jews in Judea and Samaria do not threaten Palestinians. As a general matter, many Palestinians do threaten Jews. In the rare instance where a Jew acts criminally, Israelis overwhelmingly agree (as do I) that criminal prosecution is necessary. And the Israeli government takes appropriate action.

But that's not the way the world sees it. Over the past few years, the term *settler violence* has emerged as a problem just as severe as—to many even more severe than—Palestinian terrorism. That's just ridiculous. Settler violence—meaning violence committed by Jewish residents in Judea and Samaria against Palestinians—is just a tiny fraction of Palestinian terrorism against Jews.

The U.S. State Department largely is the culprit in the development of this false narrative. Every year it publishes a "Country Report" on "Israel, the West Bank and Gaza." It's very long and hardly worth quoting here. But the overall takeaway from the report is that settler violence is on par with Palestinian terrorism—they are opposite sides of the same coin.

When I was the U.S. ambassador to Israel, it was my job to clear these reports. When I saw the first draft in 2017, I couldn't believe my eyes. You would think from reading the report that Palestinian terror and "Jewish terror" were in equipoise—equal amounts on both sides with no particular side to blame.

This just defied credulity. Everyone knows that, as they say, if the Palestinians would lay down their arms, there would be peace. But if Israel were to lay down its arms, there would be no Israel. It's not a debatable point to anyone familiar with the territory.

Why did our government get this so wrong? The answer was willful ignorance. Not a single drafter of the report had ever been to a Jewish community in Judea and Samaria or spoken with its residents. They all relied exclusively on left-wing NGO reports whose mission was to destroy the Jewish presence in Judea and Samaria.

My conversations with these State Department employees were surreal. I would ask them how they went about characterizing, quantifying, and attributing causation to the violence on which they were assigned to report. They told me they had a series of NGOs that helped them. I then noted that all the NGOs that were working in Judea and Samaria had a pro-Palestinian basis. Shouldn't they go visit the area and speak to some local leaders and get a more objective handle on the issues? Their response: the State Department forbade them from visiting Jewish settlements.

I was able to fix this issue temporarily while I was in office. I insisted on reliable data and not just anecdotal evidence from anti-Israel advocates that had polluted prior reporting. But I see now that the Biden administration has returned the State Department to an agenda-driven approach, excusing or minimizing the impact of Palestinian violence and pushing for Palestinian statehood.

The absurdity of our own government came to a head on March 14, 2024, when President Biden, in the middle of Israel's existential battle against Palestinian terrorists, decided to impose sanctions on "three extremist

Israeli settlers" and their outposts for violence against Palestinians. Yes, you heard that correctly: no sanctions against the Palestinian Authority for funding terrorism, no sanctions against the leaders of Hamas—each reportedly worth more than four billion dollars—now living in luxury in Qatar, and no sanctions against the pro-Hamas leaders infecting U.S. college campuses. Just sanctions against three farmers in a remote territory in Judea and Samaria.

I don't know these three guys. I don't know what they did. If they did act violently, I don't know what threats or attacks against them caused them to respond. But I do know this. If they were not acting in self-defense, if they broke the law, the Israeli government is both capable and willing to punish them. By injecting himself into this purely local matter of law enforcement, Biden was sending a very clear and unfortunate message: the United States does not view Israel as having the right to be in charge of this land. It was a highly insulting and entirely politically driven message.

The narrative from the Biden administration is completely at odds with the reality on the ground in the Jewish communities of Judea and Samaria. Unfortunately, American willful ignorance precludes a more accurate understanding. Since Israel repatriated Judea and Samaria in 1967, I have been the only U.S. ambassador to visit there.

Because of the mistaken nomenclature that describes every community in Judea and Samaria as a "settlement," the impression held by most people unfamiliar with the territory is that of the "Wild West"—a bunch of pioneer zealots with circled wagons and a lot of weapons, encroaching upon the natives and defending themselves when the natives resist. Those who hold this impression will be shocked if they ever pay a visit.

The largest city in Judea and Samaria is Modiin Illit. It has a population of approximately seventy-three thousand people, almost all of whom are ultra-Orthodox. The city is modern and well designed, and there is no history of its residents engaging in anti-Palestinian violence. The same characteristics apply to Beitar Illit, with a population of about sixty thousand.

Ma'ale Adumim is a more urban city within Judea and Samaria about four miles east of Jerusalem. It has a population of about forty thousand, over 70 percent of whom are secular. Again, this is a peaceful community that has shown no aggression toward its Palestinian neighbors. Another city is Ariel, home to about twenty thousand people as well as Ariel University, which includes a fully accredited medical school.

There you have just four cities in Judea and Samaria that account for 40 percent of the Jewish population. There are many other towns, villages, and local councils that account for the rest—modern communities that are self-sustaining with local schools, health care, and trade. While there undoubtedly are some lost souls within Judea and Samaria, as everywhere else, who demean their faith with unjust actions, they are the overwhelming exceptions, and their conduct is universally condemned.

We've already had a brief (but I think adequate) review of the legality of Jewish settlement in Judea and Samaria on a macro level—that is, we know it generally is not illegal. But what about individual tracts of land owned by Palestinians—are they forfeited back to Israel?

The answer is no. A Palestinian who can prove his title to a particular tract will have his entitlement recognized by the Israeli judicial system. But much of the land—and most of the land on which Jewish communities reside—is referred to as "state land," or land without a specific owner.

Many have made a career of proving, or attempting to prove, that certain land currently owned by Jews really belonged to Arabs in the past. Where the cases have clear merit, there should be justice. Otherwise, I have no patience for it. The world was turned upside down in the twentieth century, with two world wars followed by five wars and countless battles between Israel and its enemies. During that upheaval, millions were displaced, almost all against their will.

Six million Jews were killed and millions more were displaced in the Holocaust, and some nine hundred thousand Jews were evicted from Arab countries in the Middle East and North Africa. Not one got their home back! Arabs also were displaced when Israel came into existence. But many left voluntarily with the encouragement of Arab nations. Israel's Arab enemies wanted to attack Israel without any Palestinians in the way. They told the Palestinians to leave and then come back after Israel was destroyed. The Palestinians bet on the wrong horse.

Every war has created refugees. In almost all cases, those refugees have been resettled elsewhere. That includes many Palestinians. But indulged by their own personal relief agency at the United Nations, the "right of return" of Palestinian refugees enjoys international support. The Palestinians see it as an alternative means of destroying Israel, demographically instead of militarily.

There is no shortage of alleged and perceived grievances from the last century. They will never be vindicated. Life is too short, and there are just too many urgent problems that must be addressed. The Palestinians whose grandparents and great-grandparents lost their homes seventy-five years ago will need to look forward not backward. It is the future that holds promise, not the past.

Violence is a real issue in Judea and Samaria, but settler violence is a far smaller component than Palestinian violence. Over time, it can best be controlled when all residents have confidence and respect for one another and for their leadership. The future of Judea and Samaria will only be peaceful when there is a single, noncorrupt government delivering opportunity and security to all the inhabitants of this sacred land: the State of Israel.

15
THE JEWS OF SILENCE NO LONGER

Over the past seventy-five years, American Jews have enjoyed the most hospitable environment in the history of the Diaspora. They were free to believe or not to believe, to observe God's commandments or to ignore them. Some were overcome by the glory of God's return to Zion and others nonplussed. It didn't matter. In this free society, Jews could chart their own course, and they all did just that.

One thing that most American Jews had in common was their comfort in being American. From the agnostics who saw religion as a relic of the past to the overtly religious and deeply faithful, they all loved their country and considered themselves welcome to be themselves.

In the backs of their minds, however, there was just a touch of doubt. After all, most Jews know some history. And history told them that, as the Passover Haggadah teaches, "in every generation, there rises up a force that will seek to destroy us." The Jews were driven out of Jerusalem by the Romans in the first century, they were banished from England during the period of the Crusades, they were expelled from Spain during the Inquisition, they had to flee what is now Ukraine during the Cossack rebellion led by Bohdan Khmelnytsky in 1648, and of course, there was the Holocaust in World War II followed by the expulsion of Jews from Arab countries beginning in 1949.

After the Holocaust, Jews in the United States have always had that tinge of doubt. "Could this happen to us in America?" It's a reasonable question, especially given the United States' failure to protect the Jews in the 1940s.

During World War II, it became known to American Jews no later than 1942 that Hitler was executing a plan to annihilate the Jews of Europe. Some stood up courageously for their Jewish brothers and sisters across the Atlantic. Others were too timid to respond, afraid of creating resentment among their countrymen who might feel that World War II was being fought for the Jews. A generation later, many American Jews were asked by their children what they did to oppose the Holocaust. For some, it was a difficult conversation.

Of course, short of fighting in the U.S. Army, which many young Jewish men did with honor, there was not much that Jewish Americans in the 1940s could do to affect the United States' war policy. In truth, they stood no chance against the overwhelming antisemitism of the U.S. State Department.

On January 16, 1944, Henry Morgenthau, the secretary of the treasury, a close friend of Roosevelt and the only Jew in the president's cabinet, was exasperated by the failure of the State Department to take any positive steps to ease the suffering of Europe's Jews. In a manner highly uncharacteristic of his reserved demeanor, he wrote the following note to his boss:

> One of the great crimes in history, the slaughter of the Jewish people in Europe, is continuing unabated.
>
> The Government has for a long time maintained that its policy is to work out programs to save those Jews and other persecuted minorities of Europe who could be saved.
>
> You are probably not as familiar as I with the utter failure of certain officials in our State Department, who are charged with carrying out this policy, to take any effective action to prevent the extermination of the Jews in Germany-controlled Europe. . . .
>
> It is well known that since the time when it became clear that Hitler was determined to carry out a policy of exterminating the Jews in Europe, the State Department officials have failed to take any positive steps to save any of these people.

The failure of Roosevelt and his State Department to rescue the Jews of Europe, or even to bomb extermination camps like Auschwitz-Birkenau—which, by 1944, were within Allied-controlled airspace and within just a few miles of other targets—is a dark stain on our history. It prompts the question, Are American Jews of today as reticent and as impotent to influence U.S. policy against antisemitism as many of the United States' Jews were during World War II?

To put it differently, when our grandchildren ask us what we did in 2024 to protect Israel and Diaspora Jews from the ugly violence and harassing rhetoric of antisemites, will it also be a difficult conversation?

I think in some cases the answer will be no. In others, Jews will look back in shame, this time with no excuse.

In the 1940s, Jewish Americans were new to their country. Most were Eastern European immigrants without resources who spoke little English and who wanted desperately to be accepted by their adopted nation. They were insecure and justifiably so.

Today, Jews no longer have a reason or an excuse to be silent. We are surrounded by antisemitism, from elite college campuses to the halls of Congress, but we are strong enough to respond: strong politically, strong socially, strong morally, and strong financially. Jews hopefully will be silent no longer.

Some members of the Jewish community do not side with Israel. It is shocking and shameful but is part of the story of our history. In the earliest days of the Israelite nation, as they left Egypt, the Bible recounts that a "mixed multitude" ("Erev Rav") joined them. Kabbalistic sources claim that these non-Jews insinuated themselves into the Jewish nation and were responsible for influencing many Jewish failures, from the sin of the golden calf onward. Whether true or not, there certainly have been times when we have been our own worst enemy.

But something different happened in the United States on October 7 and its aftermath. There was a wake-up call for American Jews. Watching the closely coordinated rallies against Israel, seemingly led by foreign students and clearly funded by outside sources, one could not help but conclude that this was a national terror cell emerging from the shadows at just the moment chosen by the organizers.

Of course, there were lots of useful idiots coming along for the ride. It was a perfect opportunity for them to complain about being triggered and get a complimentary pass on the physics exam that they otherwise would have flunked. But it was just too slick and too orchestrated. Every person with a megaphone shouted the same antisemitic slogans, every mantra had the same cadence, and every tent was bought from the same manufacturer. Every speaker held up their smartphone and read prepared text that clearly came from headquarters.

The professional anti-Israel movement had waited for this moment. It had everything—atrocities against Jews to be justified and even praised, Palestinian casualties to be amplified and attributed to Israeli genocide, and an upcoming election as a means to leverage Democrats to embrace their cause.

American Jews took notice. It could happen in the United States. It *was* happening in the United States. Elite universities were siding with antisemites calling for Israel's destruction. They could not have cared less about the "triggering" of Jewish kids who were blocked from attending classes or studying in a library. But they did express sensitivity and concern for those disrupting academic life, threatening Jewish students, and occupying academic buildings. Heaven forbid their conduct might result in a criminal record!

Protestors never acknowledged that they were antisemitic, even when they called for Israel's destruction ("from the river to the sea") or for violent revolution here and in Israel ("globalize the intifada") or even when they claimed that Jewish money had too great an influence on U.S. politics. And that, of course, provoked the frivolous debate about what really constitutes antisemitism.

I'm familiar with all the arguments about what should or should not constitute antisemitism. It is deeply regrettable that we live in a society where only Jew hatred is subject to such academic debate. In the case of every other ethnic group, former Supreme Court Justice Potter Stewart's definition of "obscenity" carries the day: you know it when you see it.

To great fanfare, in May of 2023, the Biden administration published a report on antisemitism where it too got tangled in the minutia of definitions. Undoubtedly recognizing the political advantages Biden held on college campuses and the insatiable appetite held by faculty and students alike to vilify Israel, the report failed to adopt a definition of antisemitism that included anti-Zionism nor even meaningfully address anti-Israel activity on college campuses, which has caused the largest wave of antisemitism in recent memory. The Biden report took aim directly at neo-Nazis on the right: an appropriate target but hardly the only one. It all but ignored anti-Zionists on the left. In hindsight (and as I pointed out at the time), it was a glaring error.

My definition of antisemitism goes back to the eighteenth century, explained in brilliant commentary by the Vilna Gaon—the legendary Rabbi Elijah ben Shlomo Zalman of Vilnius, Poland—in a message recounted by Rabbi Doron Perez in his new book, *The Jewish State*. The Vilna Gaon reflects upon the great song of Moses, chanted upon the emergence of the Israelite nation from the Red Sea and its escape from Egypt, contained in chapter 15 of the book of Exodus. In one verse, Moses sings, "Anguish will grip the people of Philistia, the Chiefs of Edom will be terrified, the leaders of Moab will be seized with trembling."

In explicating this verse, the Vilna Gaon posits that there are three distinct forms of antisemitism: the first form is exemplified by the "Chiefs of Edom"—the Edomites (the predecessors of Rome)—who like Haman in the story of Purim, wished to physically destroy the Jews. The second form is that of the "Leaders of Moab"—the Moabites, whose biblical king, Balak, sought to curse the Israelite nation. Like the Syrian Greeks during the period of Hanukkah, Balak of Moab wished to deprive the Jews of their heritage and destroy them spiritually. The third and final form of antisemitism comes from the "people of Philistia"—the Philistines—who did not hate the Jews per se but focused their hatred on eliminating the presence of the Jews in the land of Israel.

The Vilna Gaon observed that the biblical periods when the Jewish nation was at its strongest in inhabiting the land of Israel—during the kingships of David and Solomon—were precisely when the Philistines were at their most aggressive.

What a brilliant summary from a period that was centuries prior to the Holocaust or the rebirth of Israel. But it remains true to this day. Ironically, the Palestinians, although historically unrelated to the Philistines, have adopted their antisemitic brand of denying the rights of the Jewish people to live freely in their biblical homeland.

The Jewish world is now on high alert. Jews may continue to debate United States–Israel policy from the intellectual recesses of their minds, but their hearts tell them something else: the hatred of many Palestinians for Jews is in their mothers' milk. It is permanent, brutal, and nonnegotiable.

Just look at the victims of October 7. Most of them sympathized deeply with the Palestinians of Gaza and the challenges they faced living under the rule of Hamas. When possible, the residents of the southern kibbutzim invited Palestinians from Gaza to their modest homes and gave them food, gifts, and work. They wanted nothing more than to live in peace, side by side, with the people of Gaza.

These invited Palestinians guests repaid their hosts by creating detailed maps of their homes and surroundings. On October 7, these maps were used to identify who lived where, what hiding places existed, and where weapons were stored. Instead of living side by side with Israelis who loved them and cared for them, they took to slaughter, kidnapping, and rape.

It's hard to sugarcoat this. Perhaps, notwithstanding the discouraging data, there are Palestinians truly desirous of living with Israel in peace. Maybe there are hundreds or thousands of them, and maybe far more. But not enough that Israel can ever trust them with a state. And not enough that Jews, anywhere in the world, can let their guard down again.

Jews in the United States will continue publicly to espouse a diversity of views. But they are nervous. I am nervous. Who wouldn't be when virtually every elite university and every urban city is overtaken with violent and ugly protests spewing rhetoric targeting Jews and Israel? But we will not be silent anymore. No more engaging in self-flagellation to prove to the world that we deserve to live. No more making empty gestures to prove our liberalism. No more bending over backward to be fair to those who wish us nothing good in return.

President Biden, seeing his political base violently oppose Israel's defense of its citizens against the Hamas massacre of October 7, has already cut off certain military assistance to Israel and threatens to withhold more. We should remember the words of former prime minister Menachem Begin to then Senator Biden in June 1982, when the latter also threatened to deprive Israel of its self-defense needs:

> Don't threaten us with cutting off your aid. It will not work. I am not a Jew with trembling knees. I am a proud Jew with 3700 years of civilized history. Nobody came to our aid when we were dying in the gas chambers and ovens. Nobody came to our aid when we were striving to create our country. We paid for it. We fought for it. We died for it. We will stand by our principles. We will defend them. And, when necessary, we will die for them again, with or without your aid.

Begin unfortunately is no longer with us. Biden unfortunately is. But we must remember Begin's words and carry them forward to meet Israel's current challenges.

Our parents and grandparents suffered through far worse than October 7. One who survived the Holocaust endured four years' worth of October 7s. And they built great institutions in the United States and the great State of Israel. We cannot and will not be "the Jews of silence" who were so indulged and so complacent as to let it all slip away.

This isn't just a battle to defend the Jewish people. It is a battle for the United States as well. No nation that has permitted antisemitism to flourish has ended anywhere but in the proverbial dumpster of history. Already, I see the backlash growing against the ignorant and hateful mobs calling for the death of Zionists. Their defeat is drawing near as millions of Americans stand up and declare that this is not what the United States stands for.

The great legacy of the Jewish nation will endure. It begins with the Bible and with our commitment to actualize the covenants of God.

16

THE JEWS ARE NOT ALONE

On January 28, 2020, after several years of buildup and speculation, we unveiled President Trump's Vision for Peace. In many respects it was unprecedented in its recognition of many of the points Israel had been making for decades with other "peacemakers," which had fallen on deaf ears.

The plan provided for Israel to obtain sovereignty over every Jewish settlement in Judea and Samaria along with, of course, all of Jerusalem, including the Temple Mount. It did not immediately call for a Palestinian state in the remaining territory of Judea and Samaria, but it did provide a pathway if the Palestinian leadership accepted Israel as a Jewish state and agreed to a series of significant reforms—changes that they were unlikely to adopt.

Even if the Palestinians did agree to everything in the plan, Israel still would maintain overall security control over all of Judea and Samaria, even in the territories that were majority Palestinian. In my mind (admittedly engaging in a bit of self-rationalization), "overall security control" was akin to Israeli sovereignty. Nonetheless, the plan did provide that if the Palestinians adopted all the required initiatives, their territory would be called a "State of Palestine."

I hated the word *state*. I pushed for other words less controversial, like *enclave* or *commonwealth* or *territory*. But I was overruled. The thinking was that since what the Palestinians were receiving was less than a full independent state, at least they should be permitted to call it a state.

I tried to sell the plan to the faith community, both Jewish and Christian. I made all the arguments you would expect. But with certain Jewish groups and especially with Evangelical Christians, we struck out. There was no way to spin a Palestinian state, no matter how impotent and defanged it might be. It was just anathema to many religious leaders.

In hindsight, they were right. It would have been a slippery slope once Palestinian statehood was on the table. Fortunately, God intervened; the Palestinians rejected the plan out of hand, and the United Arab Emirates engaged with us to begin the diplomatic process that led to the Abraham Accords. It was a much better outcome.

No group is more steadfast in its support for Israel and its commitment to Israeli sovereignty over its entire biblical homeland than Evangelical Christians. There are more than six hundred million Evangelicals in the world with the United States having the single largest proportion—nearly one hundred million worshippers with deep faith. It is the largest denomination of Christianity.

Within a month of October 7, as ugly rallies were gathering in Times Square glorifying the mini-Holocaust perpetrated by Hamas, the words "Israel, You Are Not Alone" could be seen broadcast on the largest jumbotron screen right in the middle of it all—produced and financed by

Christians United for Israel, founded by my dear friend Pastor John Hagee. With ten million followers, CUFI is the largest of many Evangelical groups that have stepped up for Israel in record numbers in its desperate time of need.

Evangelical support for Israel is not political. It makes no difference whether the Israeli government is right, left, or center. It is simply a matter of faith and, in particular, God's words to Abraham in Genesis 12:3: "And I will bless those who bless you and I will curse those who curse you, and all the peoples on earth will be blessed through you."

I have said many times while ambassador to Israel that the United States is at its best when it supports Israel. I was referring to the importance of the United States standing for democracy, freedom, and Judeo-Christian values. I always contend that in supporting Israel, the United States is sending exactly the right message to rogue nations and actors that we would never be bullied into rejecting our values or our friends. Indeed, I believe that when history books are written with sufficient time for real academic assessment, scholars will conclude that the support that the United States gave Israel during the Trump administration was a major factor in there being no new wars during that period.

Most Evangelical Christians agree with all that, with an important additional layer: they believe that U.S. support for Israel brings God's blessings upon the United States. It's that simple and that powerful! I'm not Christian, but I do believe they are right.

There's also the foundational issue of the coming of the Messiah, central, although different in religious practice, to both Christians and Jews. Pastor Larry Huch, a leading Evangelical leader in Dallas, Texas, offered this well-accepted view:

> We all know that the scriptures state unequivocally that the land belongs to Israel and the Jewish people. That's obvious, but what gets the Church's attention is that the Messiah will only come when Jerusalem is in the hands of the Jews.
>
> The most important sign from God for the coming of the Messiah is the fulfillment of God's prophesies that Israel would be restored as a nation to its Biblical homeland. No nation in history had ever returned from ancient destruction or disappearance. But in 1948, the Jews did just that! God proved that the Jews remain his chosen people and he is removing the barriers between Jews and Christians.

More than six hundred million people around the globe believe that Israel's presence in Jerusalem, Judea and Samaria, and elsewhere in the land of Israel is a precondition to Messianic redemption. No believer could possibly seek to destroy that possibility by advocating for the surrender of Israel's biblical homeland.

Even in non-Messianic terms, many Christians see the Jewish presence in Judea and Samaria as the fulfillment of God's will and something that everyone must try to facilitate.

Pastor Terri Copeland Pearsons (chief visionary officer of Eagle Mountain International Church / Kenneth Copeland Ministries of Fort Worth, Texas) makes this point better than anyone. These are her words:

> How could any sincere Christian or Jew claim to love God and not love what He loves? Few things are so

specifically repeated in scripture as God's unending love for His people, the Jews. This love is perfectly expressed through His Covenant gift to them, the land of Israel. Beginning in Judea and Samaria, He forever knit Land and people together; neither being whole without the other. No people have more right of return anywhere than the Jew to all his Divinely appointed homeland. So it is with extreme delight that the enlightened Christian devotes a significant portion of heart, soul and resources to the security and prosperity of all the Jews obeying their Divine call to the land where they truly belong.

With the convergence of faith and politics in the United States, this is a singular period in which God's will can be done. Israel, as the one Jewish state with sovereignty over all its God-given territory, can usher in a period of blessings for the United States and the entire world. Blessings, I should add, that are desperately needed!

17

THE GAZA STRIP
The Elephant in the Room

As I write this book, the war in Gaza continues to rage on. Israel is now approaching the completion of its operations in Rafah, the last bastion of the Hamas military. Biden demanded that Israel not attack Rafah—he claimed it would result in too many civilian casualties. He also withheld ammunition required by Israel to defeat Hamas in Rafah, including the very weaponry needed by Israel to attack with surgical precision and thereby avoid civilian casualties. Biden was prepared to leave Hamas in control of Gaza.

Fortunately, Israel did not listen to Biden. It successfully evacuated most of Rafah's civilian population and eliminated many Hamas terrorists. The notion that the Biden administration knew better than Israel regarding the prosecution of this war always was absurd, and, in Rafah, that became demonstrably true.

Israel now has destroyed almost all the twenty-four Hamas battalions. Each battalion consists of over one thousand Hamas terrorists. For a battalion to be considered "destroyed," at least half of the fighters must be killed or captured, and the command and control for the battalion must be disabled. This means, however, that even where battalions are destroyed, there may be hundreds of Hamas fighters still on the loose, capable of reorganizing and rearming.

Of the 250 innocents taken hostage on October 7, about 116 are said to remain in captivity, although Hamas has offered almost no information regarding how many remain alive. On June 8, 2004, Israel conducted a daring raid in Nuseirat, in Central Gaza, and rescued four hostages alive. The hostages were being held captive in "civilian" apartments, one of which was reportedly occupied by a journalist who worked for Al Jazeera—the pro-Palestinian outlet based in Qatar.

The rescue operation put the lie to the blanket distinction maintained in the mainstream media between "militants" and "civilians." Here, the so-called civilians were actively engaged in holding Israelis captive.

After the successful rescue, some world leaders lamented the loss of "civilian" life. Josep Borrell, the foreign policy chief of the European Union, called the hostage rescue "appalling" and "another massacre of civilians," which the EU "condemns in the strongest terms."

I'm not sure how Borrell expected Israel to rescue hostages being held captive in apartments. Perhaps he thinks Israeli soldiers should have just knocked on the front door and announced that they had come to retrieve the Israelis—something that undoubtedly would have led to the quick demise of the hostages and the soldiers.

Israel did what any moral and capable nation would have done to bring back its kidnapped citizens. And when they found themselves under massive fire, they fired back—with enough force to push the enemy back in order to complete the rescue. Israel acted heroically and brilliantly, and those who stood in its way properly met their maker.

But this is the mindset of idiots like Borrell, much of Europe, and many U.S. Democrats. If Borrell's family was kidnapped, I guarantee that he would be pushing for exactly what Israel achieved. His inability to appreciate that the Jewish people also have a right to self-defense and to live in peace reveals his bias. To put a finer point on this, the head of foreign policy at the EU hates Jews. Period.

This refusal on the part of world leaders to permit Israel to win this war is maddening and, ultimately, self-defeating. The Israel-Hamas war is as perfect a case of good versus evil as one can find. Defeating evil is decidedly in the national interest of every peace-loving country. Appeasing evil is a certain means by which evil will expand and flourish.

Perhaps what Borrell is telling us is that it is already too late for Europe. Its open border policy has led to large radicalized Muslim elements within its major cities. London and Paris have become almost ungovernable over the last decade. But while the EU may have no choice other than to placate Hamas, the United States is not there. At least not yet. But under the Biden administration, we are heading in Europe's direction.

Those who say that Hamas cannot be defeated because it is an "ideology" are just speaking from fear or weakness. Nazism too was an ideology; fascism was an ideology, and ISIS was driven by ideology. Of course, there are still miscreants out there professing allegiance to those ideologies. But the violent organizations implementing these warped ideologies have been defeated. Just as Hamas must be defeated.

Hamas's defeat is critical for the United States as well as Israel. With the possible exception of the Gulf War in 1991—and I would argue that the Gulf War was far from a clear success—the United States has not won a war since World War II. Vietnam, Korea, Iraq, and Afghanistan all ended without a decisive victory.

But Israel's war against Hamas is, without question, winnable. The terrorists can and must be eliminated to the point where they cannot regroup and attack again. The entire region is watching carefully to see if Israel will destroy these radical Islamists or if the United States will get its famous cold feet and push for a truce with Hamas still in control. If the United States pushes Israel into a ceasefire, Iran will become emboldened and accelerate its mission to eliminate Israel. And the moderate Sunni states will become disheartened, losing confidence in Israel as a leading partner in the fight against radical Islam.

If the United States pushes Israel into a premature ceasefire, the credibility of both countries as a force for stability in the Middle East may be irreparably harmed. For the sake of both countries, let's hope that Israel resists this pressure.

The United States also is demanding that Israel establish a "day after" plan for Gaza when the war ends. And it has insisted that the plan not include control of Gaza by Israel. The demand is nonsensical.

The possibilities for the postwar control of Gaza are fourfold: (1) a coalition of Arab neighbors, (2) the United Nations, (3) the Palestinian Authority, and (4) Israel.

As of now, not a single Arab country has offered to assume responsibility for the postwar Gaza Strip. The most likely partner, Egypt (which held the strip from 1948 until 1967), has no interest in doing so. The Egyptian government led by General al-Sisi is constantly threatened by the Muslim Brotherhood terror group in Egypt, and Hamas is an offshoot of that organization. When I was the U.S. ambassador to Israel, we pleaded with Egypt to accept workers from Gaza into Egypt for daily work assignments. Egypt adamantly refused—it does not want to absorb a single radical from Gaza.

Recently, some fifty terror tunnels were discovered connecting Egypt to Gaza. They were deep underground and extremely wide. Undoubtedly, corrupt Egyptians were paid off by Hamas's sponsors to permit large weapons to be smuggled into Gaza from Egypt. This is yet another reason why Egypt is the wrong party to secure Gaza.

The United Nations is a feckless organization that proves, time and time again, that it protects and covers for the enemies of peace. Regarding Israel, the best example is UNIFIL—the United Nations Interim Force in Lebanon. When Israel left southern Lebanon in 2006, UNIFIL was put in place to make sure that Hezbollah did not rearm. UNIFIL's failure in this singular task has been breathtaking: under its watch, Hezbollah not only rearmed, but it rebuilt its military capacity far beyond its capabilities when UNIFIL assumed its role. After Israel, Hezbollah now is the strongest military in the region.

UNRWA, of course, is the UN agency active in Gaza. As discussed earlier, it has been proven to be an aider and abettor of Hamas.

So barring unforeseen developments, we can scratch an Arab coalition off the list of future stewards for Gaza and certainly the UN as well.

Next up is the Palestinian Authority—the choice of the U.S. State Department and the White House. As we have discussed, the PA is corrupt, it continues to pay terrorists to kill Jews notwithstanding a demand by the United States that this practice end, it has no popular support, and 85 percent of its constituents approved of the Hamas massacre of October 7. The PA also has said that it will not assume responsibility for Gaza unless it is awarded a Palestinian state in Judea and Samaria. Plainly, the PA is disqualified from consideration.

Which leaves us only with Israel as a possible custodian of the Gaza Strip. No other force can protect Israelis from future attacks from Gaza. And remember, even when Israel destroys a Gaza battalion, there remain free terrorists from that battalion who are hiding and waiting to attack again. Gaza will remain unstable for years to come, and only Israel holds the military intelligence needed to keep Hamas from reemerging. With Israeli control and a complete reset of the educational system, perhaps one day Gaza can be deradicalized.

The One Jewish State agenda could play a positive role in this regard. If, through Israeli sovereignty over Judea and Samaria, Israel can demonstrate over time that Palestinians have the best prospects for a prosperous and dignified life under Israeli rule, the people of Gaza may seek that option as well.

But it is just too soon for Israel to declare its sovereignty over Gaza. The situation is too raw and difficult to predict. The short-term goal must be to restore stability and reduce radicalization. And even that could take years.

Israel's leadership today says it has no interest whatsoever in occupying Gaza. They are telling the truth. Israel is in the process of responding to a surprise attack that was enormously lethal and barbaric, and its goal is simply to defeat its enemy and restore security to the Gaza periphery. And a discussion about sovereignty now would only cause Israel's enemies to accuse it of having a secret desire for territorial gains.

This is not the time to discuss Israeli sovereignty over Gaza. But that time will come, whether because it makes sense, or because there is no other choice, or because it is God's will (or all three). Gaza is, after all, part of Biblical Israel. In the book of Joshua chapter 15, the cities granted to the tribe of Judah are enumerated. Verse 47 includes Ashdod and Gaza.

The long-term path for Gaza must be the same as for Judea and Samaria. This is God's land given to the Jewish people. Since Israel evacuated all its twenty-one settlements from Gaza in 2005, the land has been lying fallow, it has been polluted with terror tunnels and vile and despicable conduct, and it has been a source of murder and other heinous crimes. Israel has no other choice but to reclaim its biblical territory and return one day to the Gaza Strip in a manner that brings peace, not further misery.

18

WHO'S PAYING FOR ALL THIS?

In the aftermath of October 7, the financial strains on Israel are enormous. Israel historically has had a balanced budget, but for the foreseeable future, it will be running deficits. And that is before even addressing the costs of sovereignty over Judea and Samaria that I am advocating.

In the first instance, Israel must address this issue and determine whether and how to declare its sovereignty. There is a famous phrase, "Put your money where your mouth is," meaning one's views should be discounted if they lack a personal investment in the outcome they are advocating. Israel must go first. It must take the steps needed to meet its existing obligations and then to project and export its values upon Judea and Samaria under its sovereignty.

There are a number of ways to strengthen Israel, both economically and in terms of security, but the overwhelming imperative now is to rethink the issue of mandatory military and public service.

About one-third of Israel's population is currently exempt—consisting of Arab Israelis (20 percent) and the

Haredim (ultra-Orthodox, 13 percent). This was always unsustainable, but after October 7, it is nearly suicidal.

October 7 demonstrates that Israel's wars are not limited to high-technology missile defense and surveillance, where the best and the brightest within the country devise ever more ingenious methods to interdict threats from the sky. There is a need just as pressing for boots on the ground.

October 7 was Israel's September 11 beyond just the magnitude of the casualties. It also was a hard-learned lesson that the worst of attacks can come from the most primitive of assaults. On September 11, eighteen terrorists with nothing more than boxcutters brought down four aircraft and destroyed the United States' tallest skyscrapers. On October 7, Hamas breached the border with kites, trucks, and basic explosives. In Israel's case, the lesson is now being internalized that there is no substitute for armed soldiers everywhere that a threat might exist. That creates a much bigger demand on Israeli citizens than had existed in the past.

Israel is a reserve army comprising a relatively small force of eighteen- to twenty-one-year-old men and women along with careerists, plus everyone under forty who had previously served being in the reserves. The economic and social cost to Israeli society of this reserve system had been manageable, but it is now enormous. The system previously worked on the basis of about a month's service per year. Every reservist would spend a month away from his job and his family and train for a battle that was hoped to never come. It worked this way for years. But now, with changed and increased threats, absent significant growth in the size of the military, reservists will be needed for longer periods every year.

Imagine an economy where people running businesses, treating patients, and representing clients must drop what they are doing for months with no certainty as to when they will resume their normal lives. That is happening right now, and the Israeli economy is suffering as a result. Now imagine if this situation becomes permanent because of the increased manpower needs. It could easily destroy Israel's economic advances over the past decade.

The answer, of course, is to increase military service from within the one-third of the population that currently is exempt. From within the Arab community, it is essential to increase their participation. That need not include serving in a combat unit, but in a modern army most jobs do not require such engagement. Every office job taken by an Arab citizen frees up a potential soldier for active duty. In addition, increased Arab participation in the military will bring greater economic benefits to the members of the community—both direct benefits from the government and increased integration into the workforce.

As to the Haredi community, the issue is just as sensitive—perhaps even more. The story goes back to 1948 when the Haredi community in Israel was just a few hundred people. The leaders of the community approached Prime Minister Ben-Gurion with the fact that, in the aftermath of the loss of six million Jews in the Holocaust, the great Yeshivot (Jewish study centers) in Europe had all been destroyed. They requested exemption from the army to rebuild those centers of learning. Ben-Gurion agreed to the request because the number of potential soldiers being exempt was very small.

The Haredi community in Israel has now exceeded beyond anyone's wildest imagination in reinvigorating Torah study. There is more Torah study now in Israel than at any prior time in Jewish history. But it has come at a great economic and social expense.

The obligation to defend the Jewish nation is well documented in the Bible. Even the tribes of Reuven and Gad, whose territory was designated as being on the eastern side of the Jordan River outside the land of Canaan, were instructed to send their males across the Jordan with the rest of the tribes, and only after conquering the land could they then return to their families. Moses mocked the notion that these two tribes of Israelites might be exempt from military service with their brethren: "Moses said to the Gadites and the Reubenites, 'should your fellow Israelites go to war while you sit here?'" (Numbers 32:6).

The Haredi leaders would respond that they are not sitting by idly while their brothers and sisters go to war. They would argue that Torah provides the ultimate defense for the Jewish nation. But there are significant problems with that argument:

1. It is not accepted by the people who need to be convinced; if anything, this argument only exacerbates understandable resentment from those who risk their lives against those who don't.
2. Not all Haredi students are studying Torah all day long.
3. There are plenty of religious Zionists who actively engage in Torah study and serve in the Israeli military. Indeed, many constitute Israel's most elite fighters.

4. Insofar as the Haredi community has the highest birthrate in the country, this position will lead to an increasing shortfall of soldiers and an increasing poverty rate, as nonservice in the military is a key marker for economic disadvantage.
5. After October 7, the need for additional soldiers cannot be met any other way.
6. The Supreme Court has ruled on several occasions that the Haredi exemption violates principles of equal treatment under the law.

Politically, it is difficult for right-wing parties in Israel to form a governing coalition without the Haredi parties, who typically garner about sixteen seats in the Knesset. And opposing military service is their signature issue. Nonetheless, for Israel to show that it is serious about being the sovereign over Judea and Samaria, it must make the difficult political decisions to create the infrastructure for this to occur.

I remain a big believer in the importance of Torah study. It should be a national value of the State of Israel, and those truly gifted in absorbing and transmitting the wisdom of the Torah should remain exempt from the military to continue their holy work. But this is unlikely to be more than a small subset of the Haredi community. The remainder must serve their country, if not in the military, then at least in some other form of public service.

The Haredi community does already engage in significant public service activities, such as United Hatzalah and Zaka—first responders to health and terror emergencies. But the percentage of those in service is still far too small—not nearly enough to quell the resentment from other segments of the population that is ripping at the fabric of Israeli society.

Significantly growing the scale of Haredi military and public service will unite the country, it will better enable Israel to defend itself from its many enemies, and it will grow Israel's GDP so that it can finance the many challenges on its horizon. This is a key means by which Israel can demonstrate its commitment to a new future.

Israel will need other financial assistance to assert and maintain its sovereignty over Judea and Samaria. But it does have the opportunity to reposition other money that has already been committed or at least discussed.

The easiest bucket to tap into and reposition is that of the United States. It now gives over one billion dollars a year to the Palestinians. About one-third goes to UNRWA, which has been exposed as a willing participant in Hamas's terror activities. The United States should cut off UNRWA just as we did in the Trump administration. About one-half of the funds go to the corrupt Palestinian Authority, which pays terrorists to kill Jews. We should cut them off as well, again as we did in the Trump administration.

Another source of funds will be the cost of the PASF—the Palestinian Security Force. This was a creature of the Oslo Accords and manned by the U.S. State Department and the CIA in conjunction with other nations. It was designed to create a Palestinian force capable of ensuring national security once a Palestinian state was established.

The progress made in training these Palestinians has been opaque for years. The head of the multinational force in charge of the training has always been a U.S. three-star general.

I am quite skeptical about the future value of this project. Regardless of the skills that are being taught to these would-be soldiers, I question their will to stand between terrorists and their victims. Until the practice was outlawed, there were multiple incidents of PASF officers acting as pallbearers at the funerals of terrorists. There have been occasional examples of success, but they are few and far between.

An Israeli NGO called Regavim has studied incidents of malfeasance by the PASF. It has reported that since 2020, forty-six PASF members have been killed in the act of committing terrorist attacks against Israeli citizens and soldiers. The Palestinian Authority crowned them as "martyrs."

Regavim also reported that in the same period, another thirty-two PASF members were arrested or wounded for acts of terrorism. The PASF does not seek to hide this fact. Indeed, PASF spokesman Colonel Talal Dweikat has said that "for some 30 years, the PASF has sacrificed more than 2000 martyrs," referring to those who died in the course of committing acts of terror.

Recently, I got a glimpse into the thinking of the former U.S. military head of the PASF training team—General Mark Schwartz, a three-star general who worked for me in the last year of my term. I should note that I worked well with General Schwartz when he commanded the PASF, as I did with his predecessors, who were outstanding.

General Schwartz is an American hero, having served our country in Iraq and Afghanistan with distinction. But his recent public comments regarding Israel's war with Hamas were both wrong and inappropriate.

General Schwartz was not impressed with the fact that Israel killed fewer than two civilians for every killed

Hamas terrorist—recognized by other military experts as indicating extraordinary care for the civilian population of Gaza, especially given Hamas's use of human shields. He said that such metrics do not even exist in analyzing urban warfare.

General Schwartz was mistaken. John Spencer, the chair of urban warfare studies at the Modern Warfare Institute at West Point, relying on exactly such metrics regarding Israel's war in Gaza, said, "Israel has done more to prevent civilian casualties in war than any military in history, setting a standard that will be both hard and potentially problematic to repeat."

General Schwartz also recently complained to the *New York Times* that the U.S. embassy in Israel under my leadership did not do enough to curb "settler violence." I've already dealt with that issue, but his comment reveals an important flaw in the PASF training program.

General Schwartz was charged with the task of training a Palestinian security force, and he graded his performance—perhaps others did as well—by how competent that force became. He needed their loyalty to accomplish that goal, and he offered them his loyalty in return. He seemed to view himself as Lawrence of Arabia, creating from scratch the Arab Legion. This led to a myopia that focused almost exclusively on resolving Palestinian complaints, real or imagined. And it did little to create Palestinian accountability.

We can do better than funding the PASF. If the goal is to create a local police force, the Palestinians can fund that with their local tax revenue under Israeli supervision. If the goal is to defend a Palestinian state, that ship has sailed, and the PASF is likely to encroach upon the efforts of the IDF.

Reprioritizing these payments frees up about one billion dollars per year. Additional tax revenues will flow into Israel by introducing the Arab and Haredi communities into public service.

And then there are the capital expenses.

Judea and Samaria needs better roads. It needs a good local hospital or two. It needs, in many locations, better technology to efficiently enable those who do not threaten Israel to cross the Green Line to work and visit family. It needs infrastructure improvements to bring the area into parity with Israel proper. And it needs these things to create tangible improvements that will convince the average nonviolent Palestinian that a better life will exist under Israeli sovereignty.

For that there needs to be a "Judea and Samaria Trust," a fund designated for these purposes. This trust must be managed professionally by a board consisting of Israelis, Palestinians, and donors. Every dollar must be accounted for.

The trust can be funded by our allies in the Gulf as a demonstrated contribution to the prosperity of the Palestinian people. It can be funded by nations in Europe who profess to care about the humanitarian conditions of the Palestinians. And it can be funded by private donors. Many of these projects are revenue generating, and relatively small investments of equity can support bond issuances to finance the rest.

If the world can finally come to the conclusion that the Palestinian people, rather than the Palestinian leadership, are the ones who count, the status quo can change remarkably for the better. Tens of billions have been poured into Palestinian society over the last fifty years with little or nothing to show for it. A professionally managed trust will direct funding where it can achieve fundamental change.

The world needs to get serious about what is, and what is not, a good investment toward resolving the Palestinian conflict. Funding UN organizations, corrupt Palestinian political parties, and ideology-driven nongovernmental organizations is a complete waste of resources—it is simply paying ransom to terrorists. Putting money into capital projects that generate increased commerce, education, and health care, under the supervision of international technocrats, will change the world.

But the key is Israeli sovereignty. Only Israel has the institutions in place to create confidence that Palestinian conditions will improve. It is indeed a drastic change, but in time, it will bear enormous benefits.

19

WHO WILL LEAD THIS TRANSFORMATION?

For Israel to declare its sovereignty over Judea and Samaria, two political phenomena are required: First, Israel's leadership must make this decision based on a national consensus and a plan to implement all the necessary changes on the ground. This isn't simple. When I worked with the Israeli government in 2020 on the aborted attempt to achieve sovereignty over just parts of Judea and Samaria, I saw how complicated it could be. While Israel's determination can be announced as soon as it makes this decision, its implementation should be deferred until the plan is fully baked.

Second, I know how important it is to Israel that the plan be endorsed by the United States. Given the headwinds Israel is facing, it is unlikely that it will go forward with this plan unless it knows that the United States will oppose the diplomatic and economic boycotts that undoubtedly will come initially from parts of the world. I believe those boycotts are reflexive, coming from those nations wedded to the two-state solution and mourning its demise. As the plan demonstrates its benefits to the Palestinian people, and as the United States stands with Israel, those punitive measures will likely abate.

Who can be counted upon to lead these efforts? On the U.S. side, the answer is easy. I worked with a president who was always skeptical of the good faith of the Palestinians and recognized the extraordinary disparity and strategic and moral difference between the relationship of the United States and Israel and the United States and the PA. President Trump has often said that he was indifferent to one state or two states—whatever the parties might agree to. His goals always were practical and targeted toward tangible improvements in the quality of life. I believe that if Israel will support this plan, he will as well. After all, there is nothing more promising to the region than Israel declaring that it will assume responsibility for the dignity and prosperity of all who live in Judea and Samaria, including the Palestinians.

Israel will want support from the U.S. Congress as well. If this plan progresses, I hope that Democrats and Republicans will read this book. Right now, there are no leading Democrats who would support Israeli sovereignty.

The truth is that while Israel historically has enjoyed bipartisan support from Congress, that support has decisively tipped to the Republican Party for two reasons: (1) the increasing presence of far-left Israel bashers within the party led by Ilhan Omar, Rashida Tlaib, and Alexandria Ocasio-Cortez and (2) the blind adherence by the Democratic Party to the two-state solution.

In January 2024, with more than three months already having transpired since the October 7 attacks, Congress wanted to express its support for the nation and people of Israel. Every single Democrat other than Joe Manchin and John Fetterman insisted that the resolution contain a statement of support for a two-state solution. Israel was literally fighting for its national life, and forty-nine senators thought it a good idea to tell Israel to hand over strategic and holy land to people who supported its demise!

In contrast, on April 28, 2023, even before the war began, the House of Representatives voted to congratulate Israel on its seventy-fifth birthday. The Democrats insisted that this birthday note remind Israel that it owed them a two-state solution. The Republicans demurred and, with the majority of the House, the resolution omitted what would have been an intrusion and an insult.

On March 15, 2024—the "Ides of March," a day famous for betrayal—Senate Majority Leader Charles Schumer stood in the well of the U.S. Senate and berated the duly elected prime minister of Israel as he was leading his nation in the longest war of its history. Among other comments, he said the following: "The only real and sustainable solution to this decades-old conflict is a negotiated two-state solution—a demilitarized Palestinian state living side-by-side with Israel in equal measures of peace, security, prosperity, dignity, and mutual recognition."

That this tone-deaf and indefensible comment came from someone with years of government service, high security clearance, and the largest Jewish constituency in the United States tells you just how lost the Democrats are on the Israeli-Palestinian conflict.

Schumer's speech was incredibly insulting to Israel, but it broke no new ground on the two-state solution. Indeed, Ben Cardin, the Jewish senator from Maryland and former ranking member of the Senate Foreign

Relations Committee, said this in 2017 in opposing my nomination as U.S. ambassador to Israel:

> Taken together, Mr. Friedman's statements and affiliations make it clear that he does not believe the two-state solution is necessary for a just and lasting peace. I am concerned that Mr. Friedman's history on this issue undermines his ability to represent the United States as a credible facilitator of the peace process. There is no realistic, sustainable prospect for lasting peace between Israel and the Palestinians other than two states living side by side with security.

Those two Democrats are, purportedly, Israel's best friends. The calcified nature of their thinking, however, is simply maddening—truly the definition of insanity, trying the same thing over and over and expecting a different result.

A "demilitarized Palestinian state" living next to Israel—what does that even mean? Who will ensure that this state is, in fact, demilitarized? Gaza was supposed to be demilitarized, and it smuggled in enough weapons to initiate what has become Israel's most challenging war. Southern Lebanon was supposed to be demilitarized, and Hezbollah created a powerhouse of an army right under UNIFIL's nose.

And beyond the suicidal risks of surrendering this territory as Senators Schumer and Cardin and other Democrats urge, it is farcical to argue that Israel should assume these risks for the privilege of forever relinquishing the most holy sites of Judaism and Christianity!

These proclamations by pro-Israel Democrats do Israel no good. They create fantasies of coexistence in which

Israel must compromise its security for naked promises from unreliable parties. This makes things worse, not better.

Compare these statements to comments from leading Republicans. For example, on October 22, 2020, Senator Ted Cruz of Texas said, "Israel is a sovereign nation and America has no business trying to dictate the terms of any agreement with the Palestinians." On January 21, 2024, Senator Tom Cotton of Arkansas raised his concerns regarding the practicality of pursuing a two-state solution, particularly in light of the current circumstances. He criticized President Joe Biden and Secretary of State Antony Blinken for continuing to advocate for this vision, suggesting that it is both foolish and dangerous. There have been many more similar pronouncements from other leading Republicans.

In the summer of 2016, Jason Greenblatt and I were called upon to draft the section on support for Israel in the Republican platform. We rejected decades of Republican policy and abandoned a call for a two-state solution. Instead, we included language that left it to Israel to decide whether and how to propose a peace agreement with the Palestinians.

The platform subcommittee passed this by an overwhelming majority, and the full Republican National Committee gave it a standing ovation.

World opinion, however, is now moving rapidly toward the recognition of a Palestinian state. In May 2024, that state was "recognized" by Norway, Spain, and Ireland, three countries with large Palestinian populations. I wondered why these countries, if they cared so much about Palestinian statehood, couldn't have recognized a state within their own boundaries. What business do they have in making declarations about Israel's borders? Nonetheless, this is the future we must confront.

The only way for the pendulum to swing back is for Israel to accept responsibility for the health, dignity, and prosperity of all the inhabitants of Judea and Samaria. It can proclaim its sovereignty and then seek international recognition and assistance for this bold and transformational project.

We talked about how the leadership of the United States might come together to support this transformation. What about the leadership of Israel?

I will not venture into the particulars of Israeli politics. But I will offer a glimpse into the biblical notions of leadership, which remain just as relevant today.

As Jacob was about to leave this world, he gathered his twelve sons for some parting words. To his son Judah, he proclaimed, "The scepter will not depart from Judah, nor the ruler's staff from between his feet" (Genesis 49:10). In other words, Jacob was saying that the kingship of Israel must always come from the lineage of Judah.

What were the qualities of Judah, among all his brothers, that made him uniquely fit to rule over the Jewish nation? Looking back on his life, the answer many provide is accountability and humility.

Judah had many challenges in his life. Among them was the episode where he had a child with Tamar, the wife of his dead son.

Judah had three sons: Er, Onan, and Shelah. Er married Tamar but died before Tamar was pregnant. By law, Er's brother Onan was required to marry Tamar and bring her children, but he failed at his task. Judah decided not to try again with Shelah.

Feeling rejected, Tamar left for the hills. Judah, venturing out one day, came across her and thought her to be a harlot. After Tamar became pregnant through Judah, she was accused of illicit relations and brought before Judah as the leader of the tribe to be executed. Judah, now recognizing what he had done, spared her life with the words "She is more righteous than me."

Judah, as powerful as he was, recognized his role in Tamar's predicament and granted clemency to a poor, single, pregnant woman—as powerless a human being as might exist. Recognizing the virtue of his kindness, Tamar's offspring continued a lineage that led to King David.

The same attributes of humility and accountability were present in King David as well. He committed a terrible sin in his illicit relationship with Bathsheba. But he accepted the rebuke of Nathan the prophet and then proceeded to repent. Kings are not known for these qualities—but this is what made David the quintessential Jewish leader.

In the Jewish faith, we recite the verse, "David, King of Israel, lives forever." King David, of course, is long gone, but this verse means that his kingship endures—a nation-state of the Jewish people with Jerusalem as its capital, governed on principles of accountability, humility, and faith.

Looking back eight months after October 7, the one word I would choose to describe Israel's failure would be arrogance. Too many leaders thought they knew better than the young soldiers who warned of Hamas terrorists training in plain sight along the border. Too many leaders were captivated by the technological wizardry of Iron Dome and other missile defense systems or the power of artificial intelligence and big data. To these leaders, ground warfare was a thing of the past—it was our grandparents' war!

They failed to internalize the lesson of September 11, when eighteen terrorists armed with nothing more than box cutters took down four aircraft and the twin towers of the World Trade Center. They failed to appreciate the small things that, once ignored, can rise to major problems. They were woefully arrogant. And arrogance is exactly the opposite of the qualities that God wants for those who will lead the Jewish nation.

In Deuteronomy chapter 17, Moses sets forth the requirements for a king of Israel. A future king is prohibited from having too many horses, too many wives, and too much money. The king is not required to abstain from any of these things—he is, after all, a king. But it is a commandment of moderation, of avoiding excesses because those will turn his heart away from his people and his tasks.

The king also is commanded to write his own Torah, to keep it by his side, and to read from it every day. A king could, of course, have a scribe write the Torah for him. But God says differently: "Write it yourself." Again, the message to the future leaders of Israel was one of accountability, humility, and faith.

While David adhered to these requirements, regrettably his son Solomon did not. He was known for his excesses in all the prohibited areas. Although he was the wisest man on earth, these excesses led to his downfall and to the division of the Jewish nation.

First Kings 11:1–13 tells the sad tale:

Now King Solomon loved many foreign women . . . from the nations concerning which the Lord had said to the people of Israel, "you shall not enter into marriage with them . . . for surely they will turn your heart after their gods." . . . He had seven hundred wives, princesses and three hundred concubines . . . when Solomon was old his wives turned away his heart after other gods; and his heart was not wholly true to the Lord as was the heart of David his father. . . . Therefore, the Lord said to Solomon, "Since . . . you have not kept my covenant and my statutes which I have commanded you, I will surely tear the kingdom from you and will give it to your servant. Yet for the sake of David your father I will not do it in your days, but I will tear it out of the hand of your son. However, I will not tear away all the kingdom, but I will give one tribe to your son, for the sake of David my servant and for the sake of Jerusalem which I have chosen."

Because of Solomon's failed leadership, the nation of Israel became divided. As God had promised, Jeroboam assumed leadership of the ten northern tribes, renamed the Kingdom of Israel. Solomon's progeny retained just two tribes—Judah and Benjamin—which became the Kingdom of Judah.

Some two hundred years later, King Shalmaneser V of Assyria conquered the Kingdom of Israel and dispersed its inhabitants across his vast kingdom. Those ten "lost tribes" remain lost today. Solomon, for all his wisdom, caused the loss of ten out of twelve tribes—five-sixths of the Jewish nation. What was left was Judah—again, this is why Jews are called by that name.

The Bible thus teaches that failed leadership of the Jewish people—particularly in the form of greed, arrogance, or excess—leads to a divided nation and ultimately a calamitous result.

We're seeing exactly that today. Prior to October 7, national division had again reared its ugly head in Israel. The nation was hopelessly divided over the nominal issue of "judicial reform"—a series of proposals designed to make the Israeli Supreme Court more accountable to the Knesset. The divide was far deeper than what one might have expected from such a technical issue. But that was because it summoned to the surface a plethora of unresolved resentments and conflicts within Israeli society that had never been properly addressed.

It was a dark time for Israel. Many leaders of the country reached out to me during that period for help in finding a creative way to resolve the issues. I was as unsuccessful as they were.

Ultimately, the national divide came to an end, but through a calamitous result—the massacre of October 7. Most within Israeli society now recognize the importance of unity, but that recognition has come at a massive cost. Let's hope such a message never needs to be delivered again.

Implementing Israeli sovereignty over Judea and Samaria will require a partnership between Israel and the United States, its most important ally. On the U.S. side, I have no difficulty in saying that the U.S. leadership must be Republican; at least for the foreseeable future, the Democratic Party remains wedded to the two-state solution. In Israel, I will not wade into the complex party politics that produces Israel's leadership. But I will say that the biblical lessons on leadership—the critical need that Israel's leaders be accountable, humble, and people of faith—remain as true and essential today as in biblical times. Adherence to these principles is a necessary condition for Israeli sovereignty over its biblical homeland.

20

RIGHT, LEFT, OR CENTER?

Framed as a plan for Jewish sovereignty over Judea and Samaria, the plan endorsed in this book will be framed as a gift to Israel's far right. Framed as a plan by which the State of Israel will assume responsibility for the health, welfare, and dignity of every Palestinian in Judea and Samaria willing to live in peace, the plan may be viewed as a gift to the far left.

In reality, the plan doesn't fit within any of the convenient buckets by which most people assess political agendas. It wasn't intended to. Rather, the plan is based first and foremost on biblical prophecies and values.

Israeli sovereignty over Judea and Samaria is God's will and the vision of Israel's greatest prophets. Such sovereignty also presents the best means by which Israel can actualize the biblical values of respect and kindness for all its inhabitants. It also is the only means by which Israel can live in peace and security.

I saw firsthand that the United States is on solid ground when its policies align with God's will. It was the lesson learned when we moved our U.S. embassy from Tel Aviv to Jerusalem, Israel's eternal capital. In November of

2017, I spent an entire month away from my post in Israel walking the long halls of the State Department and the Central Intelligence Agency trying to develop a coherent assessment of the global reaction to an announcement by the president that the embassy would be moved.

If such an announcement resulted in excessive violence or even warfare, as the pundits were predicting, the embassy move might be aborted or even canceled. And the consequences for me personally would be dire as well. I was the strongest advocate in the Trump administration for the move, and an explosion of violence following the embassy transfer undoubtedly would have cost me my job.

After almost a month of canvassing all the military, national security, and diplomatic experts in Washington, I concluded that moving our embassy was not likely to result in violence. But how does one really know? No one can determine with certainty that no terrorist will throw an explosive device into a crowd. It's unknowable. And had it happened, history might have taken a different course.

Of course, while neither the FBI, the CIA, MI6, the Mossad, or any other intelligence agency could have ruled out the possibility of violence with absolute certainty, God can. And I believe he did through the words of the ancient prophet Isaiah.

As we were preparing for this earthquake of an announcement in the last months of 2017, I took great comfort in knowing that the Hebrew Bible hints that moving our embassy to Jerusalem could be part of God's plan to bring peace to the world.

The hint begins with what is the most commonly accepted paradigm for a world at peace. Something so universal that it is engraved on the wall outside the

United Nations: "They shall beat their swords into plow-shares and their spears into pruning hooks; nation shall not lift up sword against nation nor shall they study war anymore" (Isaiah 2:4).

These are beautiful moving words—a wonderful end state for humankind. But how do we get there? In the pre-ceding verses (2–4), Isaiah gives us the answer:

> And it shall come to pass in the last days, that the moun-tain of the Lord's house shall be established in the top of the mountains, and shall be exalted above the hills; and all nations shall flow into it.
>
> And many people shall go and say, come let us go up to the mountain of the Lord, to the house of the God of Jacob; and he will teach us his ways and we will walk in his paths; for out of Zion shall go forth the law and the word of the Lord from Jerusalem.
>
> And he shall judge among the nations, and shall rebuke many people, and they shall beat their swords into plowshares and their spears into pruning hooks; nation shall not lift up sword against nation nor shall they study war anymore.

Isaiah, who lived about 2,700 years ago, is saying something profound and highly relevant to modern times. He predicts that the nations of the world—not just the Jews—will all come to Jerusalem because it is the center, indeed the wellspring, of the wisdom and val-ues contained in the Bible. They will come to learn God's teachings and follow in his path. And then, and only then, God will resolve all their differences, "nation will not lift up sword against nation," and there will be peace.

This of course begs the question: How does a nation come to Jerusalem? But the answer is well known in modern times: a nation establishes its presence in a location by moving its embassy to that site. And so, when the United States moved its embassy to Jerusalem, it was pursuing a path envisioned by Isaiah as a path to peace.

The proof lies in the outcome: after the United States opened its embassy in Jerusalem there was no violence. Indeed, what followed were unprecedented peace agreements between Israel and five Muslim nations—the Abraham Accords.

In 2017, when President Trump announced the move of the U.S. embassy to Jerusalem, almost all the left-wing pundits predicted that this would lead to endless wars and irreconcilable conflicts. About 2,700 years earlier, Isaiah had a different view. He saw a nation's move to Jerusalem as a move toward peace. Isaiah was right, and the pundits were wrong.

Just as moving our embassy was a plan inspired first and foremost by God and his prophets, so too is the plan advanced here for Israeli sovereignty over Judea and Samaria. But just because it fulfills God's will doesn't mean that one needs to take a leap of faith to endorse this plan. Rather, as with the embassy move, God's will appears to be in total alignment and conformity with more traditional economic, security, and political metrics. It is in the best interests of the United States, Israel, and the entire region.

We have been so skewed by cable news and partisan politics that we cannot process any idea without putting it in a left-wing or right-wing bucket. Then once we do so, we praise or attack the idea because it is in the right or wrong bucket, paying little attention to its individual merit. This is how we continue to decline as a civilization and make little progress forward.

God is not on the right or the left. He has given us laws that demand both personal accountability and kindness to the poor. He offers mercy to the repentant sinner and requires justice for the cruel and wicked. God is neither a Democrat nor a Republican and it is because of his laws and commandments that our founders were able to create the American republic.

It thus is a mistake to label the movement for Israeli sovereignty as right-wing, left-wing, or otherwise. Indeed, it is not a political movement at all. Rather, it is a movement that hearkens back to basic Judeo-Christian values of kindness, human dignity, humility, and prosperity. Although many reading this book will default to tagging this plan with a simplistic label, it does not belong in a traditional geopolitical box.

21

THE HEAD OF THE SNAKE

All political, ideological, and theological initiatives—and this book arguably calls for all three—must be premised on having an adequate runway for execution and actualization. In simple terms, neither Israel nor the United States can reasonably be expected to move forward on the One Jewish State agenda if either is under fire.

To bring a modicum of quiet to the Middle East and to create the right atmosphere for an expansion of the Abraham Accords to help facilitate Israeli sovereignty over Judea and Samaria, we must address the Islamic Republic of Iran, or as I and others refer to it, the "Head of the Snake."

Iran was behind the October 7 massacre. Its senior leaders traveled to Syria and Lebanon to conduct training sessions for the Hamas attack. Iran even acknowledged that a commander of its Revolutionary Guards, Mohammed Reza Zahedi, actively planned the assault. Israel killed Zahedi while he was in Damascus on April 2, 2024.

Iran is the world's leading state sponsor of terrorism. It operates within the entire crescent of the Middle East, leading a rogues' gallery of murderers and rapists from the Houthis in Yemen to Hezbollah in Iraq, the Syrian Arab Republic, Hezbollah in Lebanon, and Hamas. If we fail to address Iran, we suppress the opportunity to bring about any positive change in Israel or elsewhere.

Iran has been a sworn enemy of the United States since it took fifty-three Americans hostage in 1979 as part of its radical Islamic revolution. In recent years, its march to a nuclear weapon threatens Israel, the United States, and the entire world.

President Barack Obama, under the influence of a group of advisors (many of whom now work for Biden), thought the way to defang Iran was appeasement. He entered into an agreement in 2015—the Joint Comprehensive Plan of Action (JCPOA)—that he predicted would end Iran's nuclear ambitions and return it to peaceful coexistence within the community of nations.

It's almost unbelievable that a world leader like Obama could have been so easily manipulated and outmaneuvered by Iran. The only nonmalign explanation that I can imagine is that Obama truly believed that with outreach and friendship, and the force of his charm, Iran would make a course correction away from its path of evil. If so, his naïveté was breathtaking.

The JCPOA was a disaster of historical proportions. Even assuming Iran complied with its terms—an assumption that proved to be erroneous after Israel captured Iran's nuclear archive in 2018—that only slowed Iran's nuclear progression by some ten years. In other words, if the JCPOA were in effect today, Iran would become a nuclear power next year!

The JCPOA also placed no curbs on Iran's accumulation of ballistic missiles nor sought to halt Iran's support of its allied terror states and organizations. Even worse, while the supporters of the JCPOA trumpeted the provisions that allowed the International Atomic Energy Agency to conduct inspections of Iran to ensure compliance with the deal, the JCPOA did not permit inspections of Iran's military facilities—the most likely location of nuclear weapons.

What was Obama thinking? No serious student of Iran and its destructive ambitions could have advocated for this deal. And yet Obama's team managed to convince the Democrats to go along, creating a self-described "echo chamber" to limit the negative reaction and to reinforce the unconvincing and stale talking points.

Of course, no one without a crystal ball could have proven Obama wrong in 2015. By 2017, however, all the wildly optimistic predictions regarding a "new" Iran had crashed on the shoals of reality in the Middle East. All the money that Iran made from sanctions relief did not go to build schools or hospitals or factories for its citizens. It just went to more advanced and lethal weaponry.

On May 8, 2018, just six days before the United States opened its embassy in Jerusalem, President Trump caused the United States to exit the JCPOA. Many naysayers around the world predicted that this exit would cause Iran to immediately increase its enrichment of uranium. It didn't. Iran was scared of Trump. Iran ultimately did begin a stark increase in uranium enrichment: but that was after Biden won the 2020 election!

Iran had good reason to fear Trump. On January 3, 2020, President Trump directed the assassination of Qasem Soleimani, the Islamic Revolutionary Guard Corps (IRGC) general who was the architect of Iran's terrorist activities and platforms. He was responsible for the deaths of many Americans, and his end was a blessing to the free world.

The Iranian rhetoric in response to Soleimani's death was not unlike its prior threats to the United States and Israel. Supreme Leader Ali Khamenei declared three days of mourning and vowed "harsh revenge." But Iran's fear was palpable. It responded with a barrage of missiles at U.S. bases in Iraq that resulted in no loss of human life. The attack did cause a number of traumatic brain injuries to U.S. troops, but it clearly was calibrated not to provoke further U.S. engagement.

Iran is a bully, plain and simple. It acts aggressively when it perceives weakness in its enemy; it recoils when it perceives strength.

Since Biden has come into office, the projection of U.S. weakness has been overwhelming. Beginning with the disastrous withdrawal of U.S. soldiers from Afghanistan, the Biden administration demonstrated a failure to stand by its allies and partners, to stand against forces of evil, and to competently execute military operations. Biden's withdrawal was against the wishes of his military advisors. He thought he knew better and rejected their advice. He didn't.

In the course of U.S. history, there have been a few iconic photographs that have captured the policies of our nation, for better or worse, with enormous impact. The picture of a sailor kissing an unknown woman in Times Square celebrating the United States' victory over Japan in World War II encapsulated the thrill and relief of a brutal war coming successfully to an end. The picture of a young Vietnamese girl crying in agony after being scalded by a napalm bomb dropped by a U.S. war plane caused a significant drop in support for the war. And recently, there is the picture of a U.S. cargo plane leaving Afghanistan with desperate Afghans hanging on to the wheel wells hoping to be rescued.

That picture has not been forgotten by anyone who saw it. It is evidence of U.S. negligence and incompetence. It is evidence that in its rush to exit a war zone, the United States cannot be trusted to protect its allies, its partners, and its collaborators. It is evidence that the United States no longer fights for principle but rather for political expediency. Biden will pay lip service to women's rights, but he will leave behind the women of Afghanistan who had begun to climb out of their oppressive circumstances, only now to be returned to their Taliban subjugators.

The United States could not have sent a more encouraging message to its enemies, including Iran and Russia. The Afghanistan debacle, coupled with Biden's greenlighting a "minor incursion" by Russia, all but sent Putin off on his invasion of Ukraine.

Similarly, with regard to Iran, Biden's policy of appeasement has made the Middle East a very dangerous place. Apart from Biden hiring almost all the JCPOA enthusiasts from the Obama administration, he has failed to impose any meaningful penalties upon Iran for its malign activity.

Secretary of State Antony Blinken has testified repeatedly before Congress that the United States continues to impose sanctions on Iran. The facts are otherwise. Perhaps some minor sanctions remain in place, but they are nothing like those under the Trump administration.

The numbers tell a compelling story. In 2018, Iran's GDP dropped more than 30 percent from $490 billion to $340 billion. In 2019, it dropped another 14 percent to

$284 billion. And in 2020, it dropped another 15.5 percent to $240 billion.

In the last three years of the Trump administration, Iran lost more than half its GDP! It was on the verge of bankruptcy. It had no outlet for most of its oil, and its citizens were getting sufficiently outraged to the point where an internal regime change was possible.

Joe Biden came in and gave it all back. Iran's GDP returned to four hundred billion dollars within the first year of his administration. The sanctions—notwithstanding Blinken's testimony—have not been enforced and Biden has made Iran rich again.

This book presents a plan for sovereignty over Judea and Samaria in a manner that benefits Israelis and Palestinians alike. I hope it gains traction. But with a wealthy Iran stalking the region and lubricating the terror mechanisms of Israel's enemies, gaining traction will be a challenge.

Step one for Israel's future must be cutting off the head of the snake. Once bankrupting sanctions are back in place, leverage over Iran will be restored. The United States has the capacity and strength to present to Iran a stark choice: end your nuclear program and your malign activity or go broke. Given those two alternatives, there is a high probability of a good outcome.

22

WHERE DO THE ABRAHAM ACCORDS FIT IN?

On August 13, 2020, a few of us in the Trump administration concluded several weeks of secret negotiations known only to a handful of Americans and less than a handful of others and announced the first of the Abraham Accords—a peace and normalization agreement between Israel and the United Arab Emirates.

Over the next few months, the Abraham Accords expanded to include Bahrain, Sudan, and Morocco. Even Kosovo, a Muslim country in Europe, agreed to normalize with Israel.

Most people were in awe of these surprise agreements. The conventional wisdom for years had been that Israel needed to make peace with the Palestinians first—a seemingly insurmountable condition—before it could achieve peace with other Arab nations. We proved this thesis wrong.

But the Abraham Accords had their critics. They received a lukewarm reception from the Biden administration, who initially refused to even acknowledge their name. Others, led by the leadership of the Palestinian Authority, castigated these agreements as an end run around their grievances.

When October 7 occurred, the chorus grew louder among the Abraham Accords critics. They claimed we made things worse by leaving the Palestinians out of the original deal. Some went so far as to say that the massacre of October 7 would not have happened were it not for the Abraham Accords.

All of that is nonsense. The Palestinians were not "left out" of the Abraham Accords. Rather, the demands of the Palestinian leadership were entirely unacceptable then, as they are now and as they always have been. That's no one's fault but the Palestinian leadership itself. Meanwhile, Israel and the other participants proceeded to make a deal in their respective best interests. That deal did not cost the Palestinians a dime or a dunam. It actually benefited the Palestinians, at least in theory, by placing Israel's sovereignty plans on hold for four years to permit further negotiations.

Equally nonsensical is that the Abraham Accords, and the prospect that they might be expanded to Saudi Arabia, are what provoked the Hamas attacks. Hamas actually had been planning its assault for years—long before the first of the Abraham Accords—and it had engaged in other attacks just about every month.

The simple truth is that Hamas succeeded in murdering, torturing, raping, and kidnapping Jews on October 7 because Israel failed to stop them. It was a colossal failure by Israel at every level—from intelligence, to strategy, to tactics, to deterrence. It literally was a perfect storm of Israeli incompetence, something no one following Israel had ever seen before. Had any of Israel's firewalls against terror worked properly, October 7 would have been just another attempted terror attack, neutralized before it became newsworthy.

Hamas exists to kill Jews and destroy Israel. Given the opportunity, it will try this again and again without any provocation. This is simply what it does. Hamas is as likely to refrain from terror as a hyena is likely to become a vegetarian.

The Abraham Accords did not set out to resolve the Israeli-Palestinian conflict. But they also did not make that conflict any worse. Many in Israel had different views from their Muslim partners regarding how that conflict should be resolved, and the parties agreed to disagree on that issue while still working together on matters of mutual interest. The construct was similar to Israel's relationship with much of the rest of the world.

We did hope that the Abraham Accords would open the eyes of many Palestinians with regard to the opportunities available within the region once optimism and cooperation replaced hatred and ignorance. In the case of many Palestinian individuals, we saw real cause for hope. But not within the leadership.

The Abraham Accords never were intended as a limitation on the rights of the Palestinians. To the extent that the Palestinians had legitimate rights that they wished to pursue, the Accords preserved them. But to the extent that the Palestinians thought that they had a veto on any Arab country pursuing diplomatic advancements in its nation's best interests, they were mistaken in that belief and obviously were never entitled to such control over others.

The Abraham Accords are not a blow to Palestinian aspirations except to the extent those aspirations are malign. The Abraham Accords foster the elevation of the moderates over the extremists—a call for civility and cooperation between nations, even when the policies of those nations do not align exactly. They are about seeking common ground rather than dwelling on narrow differences. The Abraham Accords call for prioritizing the future of our children over the grievances of our parents.

There is no question that the Abraham Accords countries in the Arab world have lost patience with Palestinian leadership. Hamas is a threat to every moderate Sunni nation, and the Palestinian Authority has proven its corruption and ineptitude time and time again.

A meeting reportedly was convened on May 17, 2024, by Secretary of State Blinken with a group of Arab officials to discuss the governance of Gaza when the war ends. The foreign ministers of Saudi Arabia, Egypt, UAE, Jordan, Qatar, and Kuwait attended along with Hussein al-Sheikh, a close associate of PA president Mahmoud Abbas.

At the meeting, al-Sheikh reportedly announced that the PA was conducting reforms so that it could better govern Gaza and Judea and Samaria. Emirati Foreign Minister Sheikh Abdullah bin Zayed pushed back and raised his voice, noting that he had seen no evidence of reforms by the PA. He went so far as to call the Palestinian leadership "Ali Baba and the forty thieves."

I have met and spoken directly with Sheikh Abdullah on several occasions. He is a serious man keenly interested in a more peaceful and tolerant world. To his credit, he does not sugarcoat the failings of Palestinian leaders. I believe that the rest of the moderate Sunni world shares his views.

The Abraham Accords could be the secret sauce that solidifies the plan for Israeli sovereignty over Judea and Samaria. The Arab partners within the Abraham Accords know painfully well the failings of Palestinian leadership. They understand that the failings are not unique to a particular leader but rather structural and endemic within Palestinian society. They also understand the power of biblical prophecy and why Judea and Samaria are so important to people of the Jewish and Christian faiths. And they fully understand the risks to the region from a two-state solution.

Nonetheless, the Arab partners want to see a resolution of the Israeli-Palestinian conflict. Its continuation over decades has resulted in painful friction within the Arab world. And insofar as no one has promoted a resolution other than the two-state solution, that outcome has been embraced by Arab leaders.

No player, however, is pushing for the two-state solution harder than the Biden administration. Indeed, as discussions continue for the expansion of the Abraham Accords to include Saudi Arabia, there is no question that the goal of the United States is to dangle Saudi normalization with Israel as bait for the Israeli government to agree to a Palestinian state. It will not succeed.

Are the Saudis wed to a two-state solution? They certainly prefer that course as the state of the art in Israeli-Palestinian diplomacy. But more importantly, the Saudis cannot be seen as less pro-Palestinian than the United States, and that is where the impetus for a Palestinian state truly resides.

There is a huge opportunity for an expansion of the Abraham Accords around the concept of One Jewish State. The argument to the moderate Sunni countries is twofold: (1) the best outcome for Palestinians in Judea and Samaria is for Israel to assume responsibility for their welfare, prosperity, and dignity—no other governing body can achieve a comparable outcome—and (2) sovereignty by Israel over Judea and Samaria is consistent with God's covenant with Abraham (Ibrahim in the Koran) and the prophecy of Moses (Musa in the Koran). Moses and Abraham are considered among the five most prominent prophets in Islam, along with Jesus (Isa), Noah (Nuh), and Muhammad.

The Abraham Accords take their name from the biblical hero Abraham, who first heard God's voice and embarked upon a monotheistic faith. He fathered Isaac, whose progeny through his son Jacob became the nation of Israel, and he fathered Ishmael, through whom the Arab nations descended.

Isaac and Ishmael were great rivals; so much so that Abraham's wife Sarah convinced Abraham to send away Ishmael along with his mother, Hagar. God told Abraham to listen to his wife Sarah, because his progeny would descend through Isaac, Sarah's son, rather than Ishmael.

God also promised Ishmael that, like his brother Isaac, he would make Ishmael's descendants into a great nation. According to most widely accepted Islamic traditions, Ishmael, as the progenitor of the Arabs, settled in Mecca after he was evicted from Abraham's home.

Notwithstanding their rivalry, when their father, Abraham, passed away, Isaac and Ishmael buried their father together in the Cave of Machpela in Hebron. Genesis 25:9 reads, "And Abraham was buried by Isaac and Ishmael, his sons, in the Cave of Machpela." Ishmael traveled a great distance to bestow this honor upon his father.

Although Ishmael was the older son, Isaac's name appears first in this sentence. Biblical commentators observe that Isaac and Ishmael reconciled in order to give honor to their father, and Ishmael allowed Isaac to proceed first in the burial process in recognition of Isaac's primary entitlement to the land of Israel.

The Abraham Accords are thus a paradigm for reconciliation between the Jewish and Islamic faiths, with each faith based in their respective biblical centers. In both cases, there is room for a thriving minority to be treated with dignity and respect. In the case of the Palestinians, that is within their communities in Judea and Samaria under Israeli sovereignty.

23

CLOSING ARGUMENT
The Win-Win Solution

Resolution of the Israeli-Palestinian conflict is considered the most difficult diplomatic challenge in the world. It shouldn't be. The truth is that it's only difficult because we make it difficult.

A square peg will not fit into a round hole. You can use force, you can try sleight of hand, you can manipulate the square or the peg or both. But it still won't fit.

That's what the "peacemakers" have been trying to do for decades in their slavish devotion to a two-state solution. Some really care about Israel's security and think—erroneously—that this is just another real estate dispute that can be compromised in a way that will cause both sides to forget the horrors of the past and live in peace. Others see the conflict as ideological but have concluded that by surrendering territory to a Palestinian state, Israel will empower the Palestinian moderates and enable them to defeat the extremists—another pipe dream.

Most of us want the same thing when addressing this conflict. We want peace, we want security, we want an end to terrorism and radical ideologies. Some of us also want to fulfill God's will. The question is how to achieve these lofty goals.

In advocating for Israeli sovereignty over Judea and Samaria, this book relies on data, not wishful thinking. The data, the precedents, and the history all help make a powerful argument for sovereignty—an argument that could be made even to an atheist.

On top of the data-driven presentation, we then overlay the theology on this complex issue. What does God want? How should we go about trying to fulfill his will? What is negotiable, and what is not?

And what this analysis shows is that, in this extraordinary period in which we live, the data and the theology take us to the same place—Israeli sovereignty over its biblical homeland.

There is both negative and positive data. Of the former, the most important is that which proves the unacceptable risk of a Palestinian state. The dry run for such a state was Gaza. With Israel's acquiescence, it became a *Judenrein* territory, entirely devoid of Jews. And it received billions of dollars from the UN, the United States, the Gulf States, and the European Union that it could have used to build a commercial paradise along its sunset-facing coastline on the Mediterranean Sea. Instead, the people of Gaza elected Hamas, choosing a radical Islamist government, and the funds were all used to encourage hatred of Jews and to invest in weapons and terror tunnels. If October 7 proves anything, it is that a Palestinian state in Judea and Samaria—a much larger area than Gaza in closer proximity to Israel's population centers—will be an existential threat to Israel. We cannot repeat the mistake in Gaza. We must admit that the experiment failed.

Adding to this overwhelming data point are several other factors relating to the Palestinians in Judea and Samaria and the government of the Palestinian Authority. Palestinians IN Judea and Samaria approved of the October 7 massacre by an overwhelming margin of 85 percent pursuant to a poll done by the Palestinian Center for Policy Survey and Research and reported by Reuters on December 14, 2023. Perhaps that says it all.

Additionally, the Palestinian Authority—said to be the least malign actor among those vying for leadership—is enormously corrupt, massively unpopular, and worse than that, employs a pension system that rewards terrorists for killing Jews (the "pay for slay" program).

The Palestinians have never governed a nation and lack the institutions, the leadership, and the experience to do so. Mahmoud Abbas, who heads the PA, was elected president in 2005. Since then, he has suspended elections and is now in the nineteenth year of a four-year term. His suspension of elections has been accepted by the West in recognition of the fact that, if elections were held, Hamas likely would be the prevailing party.

In addition to Gaza, there are other examples of what happens when Israel cedes territory to the Palestinians. In Judea and Samaria, the Oslo Accords caused the territory to be divided into Areas A, B, and C. In Area A, the Palestinians have full civil and military authority—Israelis are not even allowed to enter. Cities in Area A include Jenin, Nablus, Ramallah, Tulkarm, and Qalqilya. Although the Palestinian Security Forces are supposed to prevent terror attacks from originating in these locations, they have failed to do so. Violence against Jews in Israel often stems from Area A, and the IDF are compelled to enter to arrest the criminals. Again, territory that is barren of Jews rather quickly becomes a breeding ground for terrorism and hatred.

The wishful thinking that a Palestinian state will not threaten Israel is completely contradicted by the facts and the history of the region. No intellectually honest thinker can reach a different conclusion.

Economically, the Palestinian Authority suffers just like its Arab neighbors, unable to generate revenue beyond about four thousand dollars of GDP per capita. A combination of corruption, security restrictions, and lack of resources all contribute to this predicament. Only Israel is an economic success. And living peacefully under Israeli sovereignty is the only credible path for an improvement in Palestinian life.

In addition to hard data, one must look at biblical guidance as well. It begins with the Jewish analysis of whether it is permissible under Jewish Law to surrender parts of the land of Israel in exchange for a promise of peace. The answer, emphatically, is "no" from many biblical scholars. While there is an exception granted in cases of "Pikuach Nefesh"—an immediate risk of loss of life—that risk does not present itself here. Indeed, it is the surrender of territory that creates the greatest risks to health and safety.

Judaism is not simply a religion. It is the faith and identity of the Jewish nation that cannot be untethered from the land of Israel. While the State of Israel has not held legal sovereignty over Judea and Samaria in almost two millennia, since 1967 it has controlled much of this territory. At this juncture, with all that has transpired since then, Israel will never surrender the biblical sites that dominate the landscape of this holy land—nor should it.

To give up one's faith by surrendering the land given by God is just too much to ask of the Jewish people. This is all the more true when the demand for surrender is in favor of people with no prior sovereignty over the land or related religious connection. The sooner this is internalized by the world, the better. The world respects the beliefs of other faiths and nations. It's high time that the same courtesy is extended to the Jews.

The Evangelical Christian view is the same but rests on a slightly different theological foundation. Respecting God's covenants to the Jewish nation is integral to the Christian faith. And blessing Israel is a path to receiving blessings from God.

The data and the theology thus converge around the principle that Judea and Samaria cannot be surrendered to a Palestinian state.

Now let's look at the positive data.

Israel is a vibrant democracy with a track record of respecting the civil, religious, and human rights of its minority population, almost all of which is Arab. Most Arab Israeli citizens patriotically support living in their country, and they attend elite universities in percentages often greater than their percentage of the population.

Arab Israelis have the highest standard of living in the Middle East, contributing to Israel's GDP per capita, which is fourteen times that of its Arab neighbors! There of course are improvements that can be made to address poverty and lack of education in some Arab communities. But these are comparable to issues in other democracies and will improve over time.

It cannot seriously be disputed that Palestinians in Judea and Samaria will have more productive, more prosperous, and more satisfying lives under Israeli sovereignty. The question is how they can be integrated into Israeli society.

The critical objective for Israel is not to swap a security risk for a demographic risk. Currently, with Israel's Arab population only 20 percent of the total, the demographic risk is minimal. But Israel simply can't pick up an additional two million citizens, especially now when they have expressed a desire to destroy it. Remember, in the end, Israel must always be the one Jewish state!

The answer fits within the two principal Basic Laws of Israel: Human Dignity and the Jewish state. Palestinians living under Israeli sovereignty must have their human rights protected by law, but they cannot interfere with the rights of national self-determination of the Jewish people. That means that while living under Israeli sovereignty, they will not be able to exercise national voting to change Israel's Jewish character. But they will have local suffrage to determine the governance of most aspects of their lives.

Some reflexively will call this apartheid. All that means is that they don't understand apartheid. In South Africa, the white minority government forced blacks from their homes into "bantustans" with substandard living conditions. Here, Palestinians in Judea and Samaria will receive legal title to their homes, and they will live with assurance that they and their progeny will be permanent residents within the land of Israel. And their standard of living will rise dramatically.

The United States is not an apartheid state. Yet Puerto Rico is a territory owned by the United States whose population does not vote in our national elections. It works there, and it can work here.

The Bible provides just the right balance: the permanent resident. A group of people who, by reason of history or circumstances, cannot be full voting members of society. But their human rights, their dignity, and their entitlement to live in peace and security must be a sacrosanct obligation of the Jewish nation.

Almost every nation on earth has something akin to a right of residency short of full citizenship. To provide that to Palestinians living in Judea and Samaria under Israeli sovereignty is a win-win for all. It will solidify Israel's national security, ensure perpetual access of Jews and Christians to the holy sites of the Bible, and afford the Palestinians the standard of living and quality of life that only Israel can provide. In time, it will also bring relief to the hostility between Jews and Arabs and end the Israeli-Palestinian conflict.

Thinking back to that meeting in the Oval Office on June 23, 2020, I remember the look on President Trump's face when we explained the plan for Israeli sovereignty. It didn't move him; he wanted a win-win outcome, one in which Israel was more secure, Biblical Israel was more intact, and the Palestinians in the region were more prosperous. Our plan then needed some more work. This is where it should land.

After October 7, President Trump recognized that a two-state solution was not going to happen. This book outlines what should happen—the last, best chance for a resolution of the Israeli-Palestinian conflict. A resolution that adopts practical solutions for improving the facts on the ground while adhering to the highest standards of Judeo-Christian values.

The Middle East is desperate for a new, optimistic, and joyful path to peace, one that fulfills God's will as set forth in his ancient, time-honored texts and that celebrates the holiness of every human life. I believe this is the path.

EPILOGUE

Points of Personal Privilege

This is not the type of book ordinarily written by a diplomat. It does not attempt to be balanced or politically correct. Contrary to the nuances favored by Foreign Ministries and our State Department, I have opted instead for brutal honesty.

We can no longer afford the luxury of spin or equivocation. The world around us is burning with Jew hatred and anti-Israel bias, and those who support Israel and its strong relationship with the United States must rise up and regain control of a listing ship.

We must acknowledge the successes and the failures of Israel's approach to Judea and Samaria. The successes are self-evident: since 1967, Israel has controlled most of this divine territory, and more than five hundred thousand Jews have established thriving cities, towns, and hamlets all throughout the land. But the failures are self-evident as well. No Israeli government has ever launched a serious national discussion about the future of Judea and Samaria nor even attempted to develop a national consensus. All the while, the vacuum is filled by those on the far right and left least qualified to lead the discussion.

Every Israeli government speaks about the importance of Israel retaining at least parts of Judea and Samaria. But none has presented a vision of how that will be achieved. Many government leaders speak confidently about the permanence of Israel's presence in Judea and Samaria, but none has brought to the Knesset concrete steps to apply Israeli civil law to the entire territory. There's a lot of talk but almost no walk.

It's entirely understandable. It's not like there aren't more pressing issues competing for the Israeli government's attention, first among them wars and terror attacks. But there is less compelling political infighting that is also holding Israel back.

If Israel wants to be treated as an owner, it must act and think like an owner. Right now, the world does not respect Israel's righteous claims to Judea and Samaria because many in Israel's leadership don't respect those claims either.

Today, Israel sustains the Jewish people worldwide. And in a world where antisemitic violence is growing exponentially, Israel is the last refuge of an ancient people.

But Israel also is a creation of the ingathering of exiles. It arose from the dedication and self-sacrifice of more than one million Jewish immigrants from Europe, North America, North Africa, and the Middle East: Jews of incredible diversity of education, culture, and experience united by only one thing—a dream. It was the dream of Moses, of Isaiah, of Jeremiah, and of Ezekiel—the resurrection of the "dry bones" of the Jewish people.

To put a finer point on this, the Jews gathered from exile to rebuild the nation of Israel—religiously observant or agnostic—were sustained by only one thing: a book. But what a book! The Bible created the connective tissue, the historical foundation, the practical vision, and the essential faith to achieve perhaps the world's most improbable and miraculous accomplishment of the last two thousand years.

Now in a world where Israel is vilified for its refusal to commit national suicide, it is the Bible that provides the road map for Israel to continue to prevail and to thrive. Remember, as King Solomon approached the end of his life—about seventy-three years into his collective reign with his father, David—he abandoned the biblical mandates for kingship and the United Kingdom of Israel split apart with ten tribes destined for oblivion. Today, just a few years longer in Israel's modern existence, the same risk stares at us menacingly.

There is a clarion call for Israel to return to the book and to its wisdom and instructions. God has given us all the best possible argument for Israeli sovereignty: He gave this land to the Jewish people!

Those who have visited the Muslim world appreciate the respect they demand for their faith. Westerners who visit are expected to act accordingly, and they do. When asked why certain rules are set in place within their society, Muslim leaders answer that this is the tradition of the Muslim religion. And rarely is anyone heard to complain.

While retaining an openness to all forms of worship, Israelis need to respect their faith in the same manner. They can and should rely first on the biblical grant of territory as the basis for their title to the Holy Land. The best response to all the anti-Zionists is that they should lodge their complaints with God, not the Jews. Even an atheist should be comfortable with this response: whether the Bible is divine or just the work of an incredibly smart human, it has endured the test of time like no other and still garners the adherence of over a billion people. It is a more authoritative text than any other.

I have toured most of Judea and Samaria and visited the holy sites on many occasions. Incredibly significant places like Bethel, Hebron, and Joshua's Altar do not receive the dignity they deserve. Hebron at least has some signage, but it is reached by a narrow and occasionally dangerous access road. The other two are almost impossible to find unless one is an experienced guide or a local resident. Bethel has a couple of minor references to the biblical events that took place there. Joshua's Altar is literally all by itself on the side of a mountain.

My point is not to encourage tourism to these sites, although that would be laudable. Rather, neglecting places this important is inconsistent with ownership. It reveals a national skepticism regarding Israel's sovereignty over its holy sites, and that, one day, could turn tragic.

Jews are the people of the Book. That Book gives the land of Israel to the Jews, permanently and undeniably. And it also places a responsibility on the Jews to be good stewards of the land for the benefit of all its inhabitants, Jew and non-Jew alike. This book hopes to create a path to that outcome.

*   *   *

Writing a book about Israel while it is in the midst of a war is a risky proposition. As of the time we went to press, the war remained unresolved. The UN Security Council has passed a resolution calling for a ceasefire and an end of hostilities in a three-phase process, coupled with a release of hostages in exchange for Israel releasing dangerous prisoners at an exchange rate of thirty Palestinian prisoners for every single hostage. Biden has placed enormous pressure on Israel to end the war, while Hamas is still rejecting offers and basking in the glory of being the world's most lethal, brutal, and successful terror organization. At least for now, it is far from clear whether Hamas will one day regroup and resume its barbaric activity.

There have been glimmers of light in the darkness. Just as some were beginning to doubt the exalted skill and cunning of the IDF and the related security agencies, on June 8, 2024, Israeli special forces pulled off a daring rescue of four hostages in broad daylight, suffering a single casualty as the commander of the mission was killed. The rescue immediately was named "Operation Arnon" after the commander, Arnon Zamora.

Operation Arnon briefly caused Israel to rejoice and not dwell on its collective trauma. But not only because of the extraordinary success of the high-stakes mission. Israelis saw in high relief the courage and self-sacrifice of their youth—willing to risk everything to save fellow citizens in distress. It has been characteristic of the Israeli army every day of this war. But it was on full display on June 8.

Israeli adults have been through these challenges more times than they care to remember. And they would like to see them come to an end. But the kids, the brave men and women in their twenties and thirties are showing themselves to be every bit as courageous, as patriotic, and as selfless as their parents once were. They will never give up and they will ensure that Israel has a bright future.

Israel deserves a government as great as its people, and I see the Israeli public engaging in discourse and debate regarding their country's future like never before. I have confidence that Israel will figure out a way to solve its problems. And it will do so in a way that brings it to new heights.

October 7 was a very painful wake-up call. There's no one who doesn't wish the public jolt could have been easier to bear. But the Israeli nation is now wide awake, and it is not returning to past practices of kicking the can down the road rather than tackling challenges head-on.

For decades, it was easier to follow self-destructive policies rather than try to change them. Policies such as giving Hamas money so that it will hold back on launching rockets. Or creating blanket exemptions permitting one-third of the country to avoid military service without dealing with the corrosive impact that has upon Israeli society. Or enabling hundreds of thousands of Jews to move to Judea and Samaria without providing assurances that they could remain in their homes just as if they had bought in Tel Aviv. And perhaps most tragically, failing to ensure that every Israeli appreciates the glorious 3,500-year-old history of being Jewish and the unique privilege of building the Jewish state of Israel after two thousand years of exile.

I fully understand the desire of many Israelis to lead normal lives, to build homes without bomb shelters, and to travel the world and not be exposed to insult and hatred. I understand the frustration of so many Israelis who believe that they are leading honest, moral, and caring lives—and they are—and yet they are accused of oppressing and subjugating others for whom they wish no harm. Every Israeli wants to live in peace. Every Israeli wants quiet on their border. Why must life in Israel be so difficult?

And conversely, why were Israelis in the top five this year in the "World Happiness Index," beaten only by countries in Scandinavia? Why are the Israeli people so challenged and traumatized, yet still so happy?

The answer, in my opinion, boils down to a single word: "meaning." To live in Israel and to defend the one and only Jewish state is to fulfill God's will and actualize the ancient biblical covenants of God to the Jewish people. It is to successfully pursue a path prayed for, cried for, and dreamed of by almost one hundred generations of Jews since the Second Temple was destroyed in the year 70 CE. Who would not find pride, purpose, and meaning—and, as a result, happiness—from being placed within that continuum of history?

Think about replicating that sense of purpose anywhere else in the world. One can, of course, find purpose and meaning by *doing* all sorts of things. But I can't think of another place where that sense of satisfaction comes from just *being.*

Israel is now wide awake and thinking about how to move forward. It is considering options that haven't been on the table before because the status quo is now so risky and quite untenable.

I am not a rabbi or a biblical scholar. But I know the lessons of the Torah. When I served President Trump as his ambassador to Israel, those lessons guided me to decisions and outcomes that I believe served both countries' best interests.

To my friends in Israel and the United States, my parting words are "Listen to God." He is speaking to us through the Torah and the words of the prophets. They are as relevant—I would say more relevant—than ever before.

I pray that with God's help, Israel fulfills the commandments to settle the land and love the stranger and thereby to build a more just and peaceful world.

Appendix 1
Israeli Declaration of Independence 1948

Provisional Government of Israel

Official Gazette: Number 1; Tel Aviv, 5 Iyar 5708, 14.5.1948

THE DECLARATION OF THE ESTABLISHMENT OF THE STATE OF ISRAEL

The land of Israel was the birthplace of the Jewish people. Here their spiritual, religious and political identity was shaped. Here they first attained to statehood, created cultural values of national and universal significance and gave to the world the eternal Book of Books.

After being forcibly exiled from their land, the people kept faith with it throughout their Dispersion and never ceased to pray and hope for their return to it and for the restoration in it of their political freedom.

Impelled by this historic and traditional attachment, Jews strove in every successive generation to re-establish themselves in their ancient homeland. In recent decades they returned in their masses. Pioneers, defiant returnees, and defenders, they made deserts bloom, revived the Hebrew language, built villages and towns, and created a thriving community controlling its own economy and culture, loving peace but knowing how to defend itself, bringing the blessings of progress to all the country's inhabitants, and aspiring towards independent nationhood.

In the year 5657 (1897), at the summons of the spiritual father of the Jewish state, Theodore Herzl, the First Zionist Congress convened and proclaimed the right of the Jewish people to national rebirth in its own country.

This right was recognized in the Balfour Declaration of the 2nd November, 1917, and reaffirmed in the Mandate of the League of Nations which, in particular, gave international sanction to the historic connection between the Jewish people and Eretz-Israel and to the right of the Jewish people to rebuild its National Home.

The catastrophe which recently befell the Jewish people—the massacre of millions of Jews in Europe—was another clear demonstration of the urgency of solving the problem of its homelessness by re-establishing in Eretz-Israel the Jewish state, which would open the gates of the homeland wide to every Jew and confer upon the Jewish people the status of a fully privileged member of the community of nations.

Survivors of the Nazi holocaust in Europe, as well as Jews from other parts of the world, continued to migrate to Eretz-Israel, undaunted by difficulties, restrictions, and dangers, and never ceased to assert their right to a life of dignity, freedom and honest toil in their national homeland.

In the Second World War, the Jewish community of this country contributed its full share to the struggle of the freedom- and peace-loving nations against the forces of Nazi wickedness and, by the blood of its soldiers and its war effort, gained the right to be reckoned among the peoples who founded the United Nations.

On the 29th November, 1947, the United Nations General Assembly passed a resolution calling for the establishment of a Jewish state in Eretz-Israel; the General Assembly required the inhabitants of Eretz-Israel to take such steps as were necessary on their part for the implementation of that resolution. This recognition by the United Nations of the right of the Jewish people to establish their State is irrevocable.

This right is the natural right of the Jewish people to be masters of their own fate, like all other nations, in their own sovereign State.

Accordingly we, members of the People's Council, representatives of the Jewish Community of Eretz-Israel and of the Zionist Movement, are here assembled on the day of the termination of the British Mandate over Eretz-Israel and, by virtue of our natural and historic right and on the strength of the resolution of the United Nations General Assembly, hereby declare the establishment of a Jewish state in Eretz-Israel, to be known as the State of Israel.

We declare that, with effect from the moment of the termination of the Mandate being tonight, the eve of Sabbath, the 6th Iyar, 5708 (15th May, 1948), until the establishment of the elected, regular authorities of the State in accordance with the Constitution which shall be adopted by the Elected Constituent Assembly not later than the 1st October 1948, the People's Council shall act as a Provisional Council of State, and its executive organ, the People's Administration, shall be the Provisional Government of the Jewish state, to be called "Israel." The State of Israel will be open for Jewish immigration and for the Ingathering of the Exiles; it will foster the development of the country for the benefit of all its inhabitants; it will be based on freedom, justice and peace as envisaged by the prophets of Israel; it will ensure complete equality of social and political rights to all its inhabitants irrespective of religion, race or sex; it will guarantee freedom of religion, conscience, language, education and culture; it will safeguard the Holy Places of all religions; and it will be faithful to the principles of the Charter of the United Nations.

The State of Israel is prepared to cooperate with the agencies and representatives of the United Nations in implementing the resolution of the General Assembly of the 29th November, 1947, and will take steps to bring about the economic union of the whole of Eretz-Israel.

We appeal to the United Nations to assist the Jewish people in the building-up of its State and to receive the State of Israel into the community of nations.

We appeal—in the very midst of the onslaught launched against us now for months—to the Arab inhabitants of the State of Israel to preserve peace and participate in the upbuilding of the State on the basis of full and equal citizenship and due representation in all its provisional and permanent institutions.

We extend our hand to all neighbouring states and their peoples in an offer of peace and good neighbourliness, and appeal to them to establish bonds of cooperation and mutual help with the sovereign Jewish people settled in its own land. The State of Israel is prepared to do its share in a common effort for the advancement of the entire Middle East.

We appeal to the Jewish people throughout the Diaspora to rally round the Jews of Eretz-Israel in the tasks of immigration and upbuilding and to stand by them in the great struggle for the realization of the age-old dream—the redemption of Israel.

Placing our trust in the Almighty, we affix our signatures to this proclamation at this session of the provisional Council of State, on the soil of the Homeland, in the city of Tel-Aviv, on this Sabbath eve, the 5th day of Iyar, 5708 (14th May, 1948).

David Ben-Gurion	Eliyahu Dobkin	Zvi Luria
Daniel Auster	Meir Wilner-Kovner	Golda Myerson
Mordekhai Bentov	Zerach Wahrhaftig	Nachum Nir
		Zvi Segal
Yitzchak Ben Zvi	Herzl Vardi	Rabbi Yehuda Leib Hacohen Fishman
Eliyahu Berligne	Rachel Cohen	
Fritz Bernstein	Rabbi Kalman Kahana	David Zvi Pinkas
Rabbi Wolf Gold		Aharon Zisling
Meir Grabovsky	Saadia Kobashi	Moshe Kolodny
Yitzchak Gruenbaum	Rabbi Yitzchak Meir Levin	Eliezer Kaplan
Dr. Abraham Granovsky	Meir David Loewenstein	Abraham Katznelson

Felix Rosenblueth

David Remez

Berl Repetur

Mordekhai Shattner

Ben Zion Sternberg

Bekhor Shitreet

Moshe Shapira

Moshe Shertok

Appendix 2

Palestinian National Covenant 1964, the Palestine National Charter 1968, and Amendment to the Palestine National Charter 1996

1964

Palestinian National Covenant

We. The Palestinian Arab people, who waged fierce and continuous battles to safeguard its homeland, to defend its dignity and honour, and who offered, all through the years, continuous caravans of immortal martyrs, and who wrote the noblest pages of sacrifice, offering and giving.

We. The Palestinian Arab people, who faced the forces of evil, injustice and aggression against whom the forces of International Zionism and colonialism conspired and worked to displace it, dispossess it from its homeland to realize its freedom and dignity and who has determined to amass its forces and mobilize its efforts and capabilities in order to continue its struggle and to move forward on the path of holy war until complete and final victory has been attained.

We. The Palestinian Arab people, depending on our right of self-defense and the complete restoration of our lost homeland—a right that has been recognized by international covenants and common practices including the charter of the United Nations and in implementation of the principles of human rights' and comprehending the international political relations, with its various ramifications and limits, and considering the past experiences in all that pertains to the causes of the catastrophe (al-Nakba), and the means to face it.

And embarking from the Palestinian Arab reality, and for the sake of the honour of the Palestinian individual and his right to free and dignified life;

And realizing the national grave responsibility placed upon our shoulders, for the sake of all this.

We. The Palestinian Arab people, dictate and declare this Palestinian National Covenant and vow to realize it.

Article 1. Palestine is an Arab homeland bound by strong national ties to the rest of the Arab Countries and which together form the large Arab homeland.

Article 2. Palestine with its boundaries at the time of the British Mandate is a regional indivisible unit.

Article 3. The Palestinian Arab people has the legitimate right to its homeland and is an inseparable part of the Arab Nation. It shares the sufferings and aspirations of the Arab Nation and its struggle for freedom, sovereignty, progress and unity.

Article 4. The people of Palestine determines its destiny when it completes the liberation of its homeland in accordance with its own wishes and free will and choice.

Article 5. The Palestinian personality is a permanent and genuine characteristic that does not disappear. It is transferred from fathers to sons.

Article 6. The Palestinians are those Arab citizens who were living normally in Palestine up to 1947, whether they remained or were expelled. Every child who was born to a Palestinian parent after this date whether in Palestine or outside is a Palestinian.

Article 7. Jews of Palestinian origin are considered Palestinians if they are willing to live peacefully and loyally in Palestine.

Article 8. Bringing up Palestinian youth in Arab and nationalist manner is a fundamental national duty. All means of guidance education and enlightenment should be utilized to introduce the youth to its homeland in a deep spiritual way that will constantly and firmly bind them together.

Article 9. Doctrines, whether political social or economic, shall not occupy the people of Palestine from the primary duty of liberating their homeland. All Palestinians constitute one national front and work with all their feelings and spiritual and material potentialities to free their homeland.

Article 10. Palestinians have three mottoes: National unity, National mobilization; and liberation. Once liberation is completed, the people of Palestine shall choose for its public life whatever political economic or social system they want.

Article 11. The Palestinian people firmly believe in Arab unity, and in order to play its role in realizing this goal, it must, at this stage of its struggle, preserve its Palestinian personality and all its constituents. It must strengthen the consciousness of its existence and stand against any attempt or plan that may weaken or disintegrate its personality.

Article 12. Arab unity and the liberation of Palestine are two complementary goals; each prepares for the attainment of the other. Arab unity leads to the liberation of Palestine, and the liberation of Palestine leads to Arab unity. Working for both must go side by side.

Article 13. The destiny of the Arab Nation and even the essence of Arab existence are firmly tied to the destiny of the Palestine question; from this firm bond stems the effort and struggle of the Arab Nation to liberate Palestine. The People of Palestine assumes the vanguard role in achieving this sacred national goal.

Article 14. The liberation of Palestine from an Arab view point, is a national duty. Its responsibilities fall upon the entire Arab Nation, Governments and peoples, the Palestinian people being in the foreground. For this purpose the Arab Nation must mobilize its military spiritual and material potentialities, specifically, it must give to the Palestinian Arab people all possible support and backing and place at its disposal all opportunities and means to enable them to perform their roles in liberating their homeland.

Article 15. The liberation of Palestine, from a spiritual view point, prepares for the Holy Land, an atmosphere of tranquillity and peace, in which all the Holy Places will be safeguarded, and the free worship and visit to all will be guaranteed, without any discrimination of race, colour, tongue, or religion. For all this, the Palestinian people look forward to the support of all spiritual forces in the world.

Article 16. The liberation of Palestine from an international view point is a defensive act necessitated by the demands of self-defense as stated in the charter of the

United Nations. That is why the people of Palestine, desiring to befriend all nations which love freedom, justice, and peace, is looking forward for their support in restoring the legitimate situation to Palestine, establishing peace and security in its territory, and enable its people to exercise national sovereignty and freedom.

Article 17. The Partitioning of Palestine in 1947 and the establishment of Israel are illegal and false regardless of the loss of time, because they were contrary to the wish of the Palestine people and its natural right to its homeland, and in violation of the basic principles embodied in the charter of the United Nations, foremost among which is the right to self-determination.

Article 18. The Balfour Declaration, the Mandate system and all that has been based upon them are considered fraud. The claims of historic and spiritual ties, ties between Jews and Palestine are not in agreement with the facts of history or with the true basis of sound statehood. Judaism because it is a divine religion is not a nationality with independent existence. Furthermore the Jews are not one people with an independent personality because they are citizens of the countries to which they belong.

Article 19. Zionism is a colonialist movement in its inception, aggressive and expansionist in its goals, racist and segregationist in its configurations and fascist in its means and aims. Israel in its capacity as the spearhead of this destructive movement and the pillar for colonialism is a permanent source of tension and turmoil in the Middle East in particular and to the international community in general. Because of this the People of Palestine are worthy of the support and sustenance of the community of nations.

Article 20. The causes of peace and security and the needs of right and justice demand from all nations, in order to safeguard true relationships among peoples, and to maintain the loyalty of citizens to their homeland, to consider Zionism an illegal movement and to outlaw its presence and activities.

Article 21. The Palestine people believes in the principle of justice, freedom, sovereignty, self-determination, human dignity, and the right of peoples to practice these principles. It also supports all international efforts to bring about peace on the basis of justice and free international co-operation.

Article 22. The People of Palestine believe in peaceful coexistence on the basis of legal existence, for there can be no coexistence with aggression, nor can there be peace with occupation and colonialism.

Article 23. In realizing the goals and principles of this Covenant the Palestine Liberation Organization carries out its complete role to liberate Palestine in accordance with the fundamental law of this Organization.

Article 24. This Organization does not exercise any regional sovereignty over the West Bank in the Hashemite Kingdom of Jordan, on the Gaza Strip or the Himmah Area. Its activities will be on the national popular level in the liberational, organizational, political and financial fields.

Article 25. The Organization is encharged with the movement of the Palestinian people in its struggle to liberate its homeland in all liberational, organizational, political, and financial matters, and in all other needs of the Palestine Question in the Arab and international spheres.

Article 26. The Liberation Organization co-operates with all Arab governments each according to its ability, and does not interfere in the internal affairs of any state.

Article 27. The Organization shall have its flag, oath and national anthem. All this shall be resolved in accordance with a special system.

Article 28. The Fundamental Law for the Palestine Liberation Organization is attached to this Covenant. This Law defines the manner of establishing the Organization, its organs, institutions, the specialities of each one of them, and all the needed duties thrust upon it in accordance with this Covenant.

Article 29. This Covenant cannot be amended except by two-thirds majority of the National Council of the Palestine Liberation Organization in a special session called for this purpose.

1968

Palestine Liberation Organization: The Palestine National Charter

1. This Charter shall be known as "The Palestine National Charter." (Al-Mithaq Al-Watanee Al-Philisteeni)

Articles of the Charter:

Article 1: Palestine is the homeland of the Arab Palestinian people; it is an indivisible part of the greater Arab homeland, and the Palestinian people are an integral part of the Arab nation.

Article 2: Palestine, with the boundaries it had during the British Mandate, is an indivisible territorial unit.

Article 3: The Palestinian Arab people possess the legal right to their homeland and to self-determination after the completion of the liberation of their country in accordance with their wishes and entirely of their own accord and will.

Article 4: The Palestinian identity is a genuine, essential, and inherent characteristic; it is transmitted from fathers to children. The Zionist occupation and the dispersal of the Palestinian Arab people, through the disasters which befell them, do not make them lose their Palestinian identity and their membership in the Palestinian community, nor do they negate them.

Article 5: The Palestinians are those Arab nationals who, until 1947, normally resided in Palestine regardless of whether they were evicted from it or stayed there. Anyone born, after that date, of a Palestinian father—whether in Palestine or outside it—is also a Palestinian.

Article 6: The Jews who had normally resided in Palestine until the beginning of the Zionist invasion are considered Palestinians.

Article 7: There is a Palestinian community and that it has material, spiritual, and historical connection with Palestine are indisputable facts. It is a national duty to bring up individual Palestinians in an Arab revolutionary manner. All means of information and education must be adopted in order to acquaint the Palestinian with his country in the most profound manner, both spiritual and material, that is possible. He must be prepared for the armed struggle and ready to sacrifice his wealth and his life in order to win back his homeland and bring about its liberation.

Article 8: The phase in their history, through which the Palestinian people are now living, is that of national (watani) struggle for the liberation of Palestine. Thus the conflicts among the Palestinian national forces are secondary, and should be ended for the sake of the basic conflict that exists between the forces of Zionism and of colonialism on the one hand, and the Palestinian Arab people on the other. On this basis the Palestinian masses, regardless of whether they are residing in the national homeland or in Diaspora (mahajir) constitute—both their organizations and the individuals—one national front working for the retrieval of Palestine and its liberation through armed struggle.

Article 9: Armed struggle is the only way to liberate Palestine. This is the overall strategy, not merely a tactical phase. The Palestinian Arab people assert their absolute determination and firm resolution to continue their armed struggle and to work for an armed popular revolution for the liberation of their country and their return to it. They also assert their right to normal life in Palestine and to exercise their right to self-determination and sovereignty over it.

Article 10: Commando (Feday'ee) action constitutes the nucleus of the Palestinian popular liberation war. This requires its escalation, comprehensiveness, and the mobilization of all the Palestinian popular and educational efforts and their organization and involvement in the armed Palestinian revolution. It also requires the achieving of unity for the national (watani) struggle among the different groupings of the Palestinian people, and between the Palestinian people and the Arab masses, so as to secure the continuation of the revolution, its escalation, and victory.

Article 11: Palestinians have three mottoes: national unity, national (al-qawmiyya) mobilization, and liberation.

Article 12: The Palestinian Arab people believe in Arab unity. In order to contribute their share toward the attainment of that objective, however, they must, at the present stage of their struggle, safeguard their Palestinian identity and develop their consciousness of that identity, oppose any plan that may dissolve or impair it.

Article 13: Arab unity and the liberation of Palestine are two complementary goals, the attainment of either of which facilitates the attainment of the other. Thus, Arab unity leads to the liberation of Palestine, the liberation of Palestine leads to Arab unity; and the work toward the realization of one objective proceeds side by side with work toward the realization of the other.

Article 14: The destiny of the Arab Nation, and indeed Arab existence itself, depend upon the destiny of the Palestinian cause. From this interdependence springs the Arab nation's pursuit of, and striving for, the liberation of Palestine. The people of Palestine play the role of the vanguard in the realization of this sacred (qawmi) goal.

Article 15: The liberation of Palestine, from an Arab viewpoint, is a national (qawmi) duty and it attempts to repel the Zionist and imperialist aggression against the Arab homeland, and aims at the elimination of Zionism in Palestine. Absolute responsibility for this falls upon the Arab nation—peoples and governments—with the Arab people of Palestine in the vanguard. Accordingly, the Arab nation must mobilize all its military, human, moral, and spiritual capabilities to participate actively with the Palestinian people in the liberation of Palestine. It must, particularly, in the phase of the armed Palestinian revolution, offer and furnish the Palestinian people with all possible help, and material and human support, and make available to them the means and opportunities that will enable them to continue to carry out their leading role in the armed revolution, until they liberate their homeland.

Article 16: The liberation of Palestine, from a spiritual viewpoint, will provide the Holy Land with an atmosphere of safety and tranquillity, which in turn will safeguard the country's religious sanctuaries and guarantee freedom of worship and of visit to all, without discrimination of race, color, language, or religion. Accordingly, the Palestinian people look to all spiritual forces in the world for support.

Article 17: The liberation of Palestine, from a human point of view, will restore to the Palestinian individual his dignity, pride, and freedom. Accordingly, the Palestinian Arab people look forward to the support of all those who believe in the dignity of man and his freedom in the world.

Article 18: The liberation of Palestine, from an international point of view, is a defensive action necessitated by the demands of self-defense. Accordingly, the Palestinian people, desirous as they are of the friendship of all people, look to freedom-loving and peace-loving states for support in order to restore their legitimate rights in Palestine, to re-establish peace and security in the country, and to enable its people to exercise national sovereignty and freedom.

Article 19: The partition of Palestine in 1947, and the establishment of the state of Israel are entirely illegal, regardless of the passage of time, because they were contrary to the will of the Palestinian people and its natural right in their homeland, and were inconsistent with the principles embodied in the Charter of the United Nations, particularly the right to self-determination.

Article 20: The Balfour Declaration, the Palestine Mandate, and everything that has been based on them, are deemed null and void. Claims of historical or religious ties of Jews with Palestine are incompatible with the facts of history and the conception of what constitutes statehood. Judaism, being a religion, is not an independent nationality. Nor do Jews constitute a single nation with an identity of their own; they are citizens of the states to which they belong.

Article 21: The Arab Palestinian people, expressing themselves by armed Palestinian revolution, reject all solutions which are substitutes for the total liberation of Palestine and reject all proposals aimed at the liquidation of the Palestinian cause, or at its internationalization.

Article 22: Zionism is a political movement organically associated with international imperialism and antagonistic to all action for liberation and to progressive movements in the world. It is racist and fanatic in its nature, aggressive, expansionist and colonial in its aims, and fascist in its methods. Israel is the instrument of the Zionist movement, and the geographical base for world imperialism placed strategically in the midst of the Arab homeland to combat the hopes of the Arab nation for liberation, unity, and progress. Israel is a constant source of threat vis-à-vis peace in the Middle East and the whole world. Since liberation of Palestine will destroy the Zionist and imperialist presence and will contribute to the establishment of peace in the Middle East. That is why the Palestinian people look to the progressive and peaceful forces and urge them all, irrespective of their affiliations and beliefs, to offer the Palestinian people all aid and support in their just struggle for the liberation of their homeland.

Article 23: The demand of security and peace, as well as the demand of right and justice, require all states to consider Zionism an illegitimate movement, to outlaw its existence, and to ban its operations, in order that friendly relations among peoples may be preserved, and the loyalty of citizens to their respective homelands safeguarded.

Article 24: The Palestinian people believe in the principles of justice, freedom, sovereignty, self-determination, human dignity, and the right of peoples to exercise them.

Article 25: For the realization of the goals of this Charter and its principles, the Palestine Liberation Organization will perform its role in the liberation of Palestine.

Article 26: The Palestine Liberation Organization, the representative of the Palestinian revolutionary forces, is responsible for the Palestinian Arab peoples movement in its struggle—to retrieve its homeland, liberate and return to it and exercise the right to self-determination in it—in all military, political, and financial fields and also for whatever may be required by the Palestinian cause on the inter-Arab and international levels.

Article 27: The Palestine Liberation Organization shall cooperate with all Arab states, each according to its potentialities; and will adopt a neutral policy among them in light of the requirements of the battle of liberation; and on this basis does not interfere in the internal affairs of any Arab state.

Article 28: The Palestinian Arab people assert the genuineness and independence of their national revolution and reject all forms of intervention, trusteeship, and subordination.

Article 29: The Palestinian people possess the fundamental and genuine legal right to liberate and retrieve their homeland. The Palestinian people determine their attitude toward all states and forces on the basis of the stands they adopt vis-à-vis the Palestinian revolution to fulfill the aims of the Palestinian people.

Article 30: Fighters and carriers of arms in the war of liberation are the nucleus of the popular army which will be the protective force for the gains of the Palestinian Arab people.

Article 31: This Organization shall have a flag, an oath of allegiance, and an anthem. All this shall be decided upon in accordance with a special law.

Article 32: A law, known as the Basic Statute of the Palestine Liberation Organization, shall be annexed to this Covenant. It will lay down the manner in which the Organization, and its organs and institutions, shall be constituted; the respective competence of each; and the requirements of its obligation under the Charter.

Article 33: This Charter shall not be amended save by [vote of] a majority of two-thirds of the total membership of the National Council of the Palestine Liberation Organization [taken] at a special session convened for that purpose.

1996

Amendment to the Palestine National Charter

The Palestinian National Council, at its 21st session held in the city of Gaza,

Emanating from the Declaration of Independence and the Political Statement adopted at its 19th session held in Algiers on 15 November 1988, which affirmed the resolution of conflicts by peaceful means and accepted the two states solution,

And based on the introduction of the Declaration of Principles signed in Washington D.C. on 13 September 1993, which included the agreement of both sides to put an end to decades of confrontation and conflict and to live in peaceful coexistence, mutual dignity and security, while recognizing their mutual legitimate and political right,

And reaffirming their desire to achieve a just, lasting and comprehensive peace settlement and historic reconciliation through the agreed political process,

And based on international legitimacy represented by the United Nations resolutions relevant to the Palestinian question, including those relating to Jerusalem, refugees and settlements, and the other issues of the permanent status and the implementation of Security Council Resolutions 242 and 338,

And affirming the adherence of the Palestine Liberation Organization to its commitments deriving from the D.O.P. (Oslo 1), the Provisional Cairo Agreement, the Letter of Mutual Recognition on 9 and 19 September 1993, the Israeli-Palestinian Interim Agreement on the West Bank and Gaza Strip (Oslo 2) signed in Washington D.C. on 28 September 1995, and reconfirm the resolution of the Central Council of the P.L.O. adopted in October 1993, which approved the Oslo Agreement and all its annexes,

And based on the principles which constituted the foundation of the Madrid Peace Conference and the Washington Negotiations, decides:

1. The Palestinian National Charter is hereby amended by canceling the articles that are contrary to the letters exchanged the P.L.O. and the Government of Israel 9–10 September 1993.
2. Assigns its legal committee with the task of redrafting the Palestinian National Charter in order to present it to the first session of the Palestinian Central Council.

Gaza, 22–25 April 1996.

Appendix 3

Israeli Basic Law of Human Dignity 1992

Basic Law: Human Dignity and Liberty (Originally adopted in 5752–1992)

BASIC PRINCIPLES (AMENDMENT NO. 1)

1. The basic human rights in Israel are based on the recognition of the value of the human being, the sanctity of his life, and his being a free person, and they shall be upheld in the spirit of the principles included in the Declaration of the Establishment of the State of Israel.

PURPOSE

1a. The purpose of this Basic Law is to protect human dignity and liberty, in order to embed the values of the State of Israel as a Jewish and democratic state, in a basic law.

PRESERVATION OF LIFE, BODY AND DIGNITY

2. One should not violate the life, body, or dignity of a human being as such.

PROTECTION OF PROPERTY

3. The property of a human being shall not be violated.

PROTECTION OF LIFE, BODY AND DIGNITY

4. Every human being is entitled to protection of his life, body and dignity.

PERSONAL LIBERTY

5. The liberty of a human being shall not be taken or restricted, by means of imprisonment, detention, extradition, or in any other manner.

DEPARTURE FROM THE STATE OF ISRAEL, AND

6. (a) Every person is free to exit Israel.

ENTRY TO IT

(b) Every Israeli citizen who is abroad is entitled to enter Israel.

PRIVACY AND INTIMACY

7. (a) Every person has a right to privacy and to inti-
        macy in his life.
    (b) There shall be no entry into the private
        premises of a person, without his permission.
    (c) No search shall be held on the private prem-
        ises of a person, upon his body, in his body, or
        among his private effects.
    (d) The confidentiality of conversation of a person,
        his writings or his records shall not be violated.

VIOLATION OF RIGHTS (AMENDMENT NO. 1)

8. One is not to violate the rights accorded by this
    Basic Law save by means of a law that corresponds
    to the values of the State of Israel, which serves an
    appropriate purpose, and to an extent that does not
    exceed what is required, or on the basis of a law, as
    aforementioned, by force of an explicit authoriza-
    tion therein.

RESERVATION REGARDING
THE SECURITY FORCES

9. The rights of persons serving in the Israel Defense
    Forces, the Israel Police, the Prisons Service, and
    other security organizations of the State, shall not
    be limited under this Basic Law, nor shall these
    rights be subject to conditions, save by virtue of a
    law, or by regulation enacted by virtue of a law, and
    to an extent that does not exceed what is required
    by the essence and nature of the service.

RETENTION OF LAWS

10. This Basic Law shall not affect the validity of any law that existed prior to the inception of the Basic Law.

APPLICABILITY

11. Each and every government authority is obliged to respect the rights in accordance with this Basic Law.

STABILITY OF THE LAW

12. Emergency regulations do not have the power to change this Basic Law, to temporarily suspend it, or to lay down conditions to it. However, when a state of emergency exists in the State, by virtue of a declaration under article 9 of the Law and Administration Ordinance 5708–1948, emergency regulations may be enacted on the basis of the said article, that will involve denial or limitation of rights under this Basic Law, provided that the denial or limitation shall be for a worthy purpose, and for a period and an extent that do not exceed the required.

Basic Law: Israel as the Nation-State of the Jewish People (Originally adopted in 5778–2018)

BASIC PRINCIPLES

1. (a) The Land of Israel is the historical homeland of the Jewish People, in which the State of Israel was established.
   (b) The State of Israel is the nation state of the Jewish People in which it realizes its natural, cultural, religious and historical right to self-determination.
   (c) The realization of the right to national self-determination in the State of Israel is exclusive to the Jewish People.

THE SYMBOLS OF THE STATE

2. (a) The name of the State is "Israel".
   (b) The State flag is white, with two light-blue stripes close to the edges, and a light-blue Star of David in the centre.

(c) The State emblem is a seven-branched meno-rah with olive leaves on both sides, and the word "Israel" beneath it.

(d) The national anthem is "Hatikvah".

(e) Details regarding the State symbols shall be prescribed by law.

THE CAPITAL OF THE STATE

3. The complete and united Jerusalem is the capital of Israel.

LANGUAGE

4. (a) Hebrew is the language of the State.

(b) Arabic has a special status in the State. Regulation of the use of Arabic in state institutions or in contacts with them shall be prescribed by law.

(c) Nothing in this article shall compromise the status given to the Arabic language in practice, before this basic-law came into force.

INGATHERING OF THE EXILES

5. The State shall be open to Jewish immigration, and the ingathering of the exiles.

THE CONNECTION TO THE JEWISH PEOPLE

6. (a) The State shall strive to secure the welfare of members of the Jewish People and of its citizens,

who are in straits and in captivity, due to their Jewishness or due to their citizenship.

(b) The State shall act in the Diaspora, to strengthen the affinity between the State and members of the Jewish People.

(c) The State shall act to preserve the cultural, historical, and religious heritage of the Jewish People among Jews of the Diaspora.

JEWISH SETTLEMENT

7. The State views the development of Jewish settlement as a national value, and shall act to encourage and promote its establishment and consolidation.

OFFICIAL CALENDAR

8. The Hebrew calendar is the official calendar of the State, and side by side with it, the Gregorian calendar shall be used as an official calendar. The use of the Hebrew calendar and the Gregorian calendar shall be prescribed by law.

INDEPENDENCE DAY AND MEMORIAL DAYS

9. (a) Independence Day is the official national holiday of the State.

(b) Memorial Day for the Fallen in Israel's Wars, and the Remembrance Day for the Holocaust and Martyrdom, are official memorial days of the State.

DAYS OF REST AND STATUTORY HOLIDAYS

10. The Sabbath and the Jewish holidays are the established days of rest in the State. Those who are not Jewish have the right to keep days of rest on their days of rest and holidays. Details regarding this matter shall be prescribed by law.

RIGIDITY

11. This basic-law may not be changed save by means of a basic-law, adopted by a majority of the Knesset Members.

Appendix 5
Pompeo Doctrine 2019

Secretary Michael R. Pompeo Remarks to the Press

REMARKS TO THE PRESS

MICHAEL R. POMPEO, SECRETARY OF STATE

PRESS BRIEFING ROOM

WASHINGTON, D.C.

NOVEMBER 18, 2019

Turning now to Israel, the Trump administration is reversing the Obama administration's approach towards Israeli settlements.

U.S. public statements on settlement activities in the West Bank have been inconsistent over decades. In 1978, the Carter administration categorically concluded that Israel's establishment of civilian settlements was inconsistent with international law. However, in 1981, President Reagan disagreed with that conclusion and stated that he didn't believe that the settlements were inherently illegal.

Subsequent administrations recognized that unrestrained settlement activity could be an obstacle to peace, but they wisely and prudently recognized that dwelling on legal positions didn't advance peace. However, in December 2016, at the very end of the previous administration, Secretary Kerry changed decades of this careful, bipartisan approach by publicly reaffirming the supposed illegality of settlements.

After carefully studying all sides of the legal debate, this administration agrees with President Reagan. The establishment of Israeli civilian settlements in the West Bank is not per se inconsistent with international law.

I want to emphasize several important considerations.

First, look, we recognize that—as Israeli courts have—the legal conclusions relating to individual settlements must depend on an assessment of specific facts and circumstances on the ground. Therefore, the United States Government is expressing no view on the legal status of any individual settlement.

The Israeli legal system affords an opportunity to challenge settlement activity and assess humanitarian considerations connected to it. Israeli courts have confirmed the legality of certain settlement activities and has concluded that others cannot be legally sustained.

Second, we are not addressing or prejudging the ultimate status of the West Bank. This is for the Israelis and the Palestinians to negotiate. International law does not compel a particular outcome, nor create any legal obstacle to a negotiated resolution.

Third, the conclusion that we will no longer recognize Israeli settlements as per se inconsistent with international law is based on the unique facts, history, and circumstances presented by the establishment of civilian settlements in the West Bank. Our decision today does not prejudice or decide legal conclusions regarding situations in any other parts of the world.

And finally—finally—calling the establishment of civilian settlements inconsistent with international law hasn't worked. It hasn't advanced the cause of peace.

The hard truth is there will never be a judicial resolution to the conflict, and arguments about who is right and wrong as a matter of international law will not bring peace. This is a complex political problem that can only be solved by negotiations between the Israelis and the Palestinians.

The United States remains deeply committed to helping facilitate peace, and I will do everything I can to help this cause. The United States encourages the Israelis and the Palestinians to resolve the status of Israeli settlements in the West Bank in any final status negotiations.

And further, we encourage both sides to find a solution that promotes, protects the security and welfare of Palestinians and Israelis alike.

Appendix 6

Abraham Accords Declaration 2020

Tuesday, Sept. 15, 2020

The Abraham Accords Declaration:

We, the undersigned, recognize the importance of maintaining and strengthening peace in the Middle East and around the world based on mutual understanding and coexistence, as well as respect for human dignity and freedom, including religious freedom.

We encourage efforts to promote interfaith and intercultural dialogue to advance a culture of peace among the three Abrahamic religions and all humanity.

We believe that the best way to address challenges is through cooperation and dialogue and that developing friendly relations among States advances the interests of lasting peace in the Middle East and around the world.

We seek tolerance and respect for every person in order to make this world a place where all can enjoy a life of dignity and hope, no matter their race, faith or ethnicity.

We support science, art, medicine, and commerce to inspire humankind, maximize human potential and bring nations closer together.

We seek to end radicalization and conflict to provide all children a better future.

We pursue a vision of peace, security, and prosperity in the Middle East and around the world.

In this spirit, we warmly welcome and are encouraged by the progress already made in establishing diplomatic relations between Israel and its neighbors in the region under the principles of the Abraham Accords. We are encouraged by the ongoing efforts to consolidate and expand such friendly relations based on shared interests and a shared commitment to a better future.

Signed:

President Donald J. Trump
Israeli Prime Minister Benjamin Netanyahu
Minister of Foreign Affairs of Bahrain
Dr. Abdullatif bin Rashid Al Zayani
Minister of Foreign Affairs for the United Arab
Emirates Abdullah bin Zayed Al Nahyan

Appendix 7
Abraham Accords
Peace Agreements 2020

ABRAHAM ACCORDS PEACE AGREEMENT:
TREATY OF PEACE, DIPLOMATIC RELATIONS AND
FULL NORMALIZATION
BETWEEN
THE UNITED ARAB EMIRATES
AND
THE STATE OF ISRAEL

The Government of the United Arab Emirates and the Government of the State of Israel (hereinafter, the "Parties")

Aspiring to realize the vision of a Middle East region that is stable, peaceful and prosperous, for the benefit of all States and peoples in the region;

Desiring to establish peace, diplomatic and friendly relations, co-operation and full normalization of ties between them and their peoples, in accordance with this Treaty, and to chart together a new path to unlock the vast potential of their countries and of the region;

Reaffirming the "Joint Statement of the United States, the State of Israel, and the United Arab Emirates" (the "Abraham Accords"), dated 13 August 2020;

Believing that the further development of friendly relations meets the interests of lasting peace in the Middle East and that challenges can only be effectively addressed by cooperation and not by conflict;

Determined to ensure lasting peace, stability, security and prosperity for both their States and to develop and enhance their dynamic and innovative economies;

Reaffirming their shared commitment to normalize relations and promote stability through diplomatic engagement, increased economic cooperation and other close coordination;

Reaffirming also their shared belief that the establishment of peace and full normalization between them can help transform the Middle East by spurring economic growth, enhancing technological innovation and forging closer people-to-people relations;

Recognizing that the Arab and Jewish peoples are descendants of a common ancestor, Abraham, and inspired, in that spirit, to foster in the Middle East a reality in which Muslims, Jews, Christians and peoples of all faiths, denominations, beliefs and nationalities live in, and are committed to, a spirit of coexistence, mutual understanding and mutual respect;

Recalling the reception held on January 28, 2020, at which President Trump presented his Vision for Peace, and committing to continuing their efforts to achieve a just, comprehensive, realistic and enduring solution to the Israeli-Palestinian conflict;

Recalling the Treaties of Peace between the State of Israel and the Arab Republic of Egypt and between the

State of Israel and the Hashemite Kingdom of Jordan, and committed to working together to realize a negotiated solution to the Israeli-Palestinian conflict that meets the legitimate needs and aspirations of both peoples, and to advance comprehensive Middle East peace, stability and prosperity;

Emphasizing the belief that the normalization of Israeli and Emirati relations is in the interest of both peoples and contributes to the cause of peace in the Middle East and the world;

Expressing deep appreciation to the United States for its profound contribution to this historic achievement;

Have agreed as follows:

1. **Establishment of Peace, Diplomatic Relations and Normalization**: Peace, diplomatic relations and full normalization of bilateral ties are hereby established between the United Arab Emirates and the State of Israel.

2. **General Principles**: The Parties shall be guided in their relations by the provisions of the Charter of the United Nations and the principles of international law governing relations among States. In particular, they shall recognize and respect each other's sovereignty and right to live in peace and security, develop friendly relations of cooperation between them and their peoples, and settle all disputes between them by peaceful means.

3. **Establishment of Embassies**: The Parties shall exchange resident ambassadors as soon as practicable after the signing of this Treaty, and shall conduct diplomatic and consular relations in accordance with the applicable rules of international law.

4. **Peace and Stability**: The Parties shall attach profound importance to mutual understanding, cooperation and coordination between them in the spheres of peace and stability, as a fundamental pillar of their relations and as a means for enhancing those spheres in the Middle East as a whole. They undertake to take the necessary steps to prevent any terrorist or hostile activities against each other on or from their respective Territories, as well as deny any support for such activities abroad or allowing such support on or from their respective territories. Recognizing the new era of peace and friendly relations between them, as well as the centrality of stability to the well-being of their respective peoples and of the region, the Parties undertake to consider and discuss these matters regularly, and to conclude detailed agreements and arrangements on coordination and cooperation.

5. **Cooperation and Agreements in Other Spheres:** **As** an integral part of their commitment to peace, prosperity, diplomatic and friendly relations, cooperation and full normalization, the Parties shall work to advance the cause of peace, stability and prosperity throughout the Middle East, and to unlock the great potential of their countries and of the region. For such purposes, the Parties shall conclude bilateral agreements in the following spheres at the earliest practicable date, as well as in other spheres of mutual interest as may be agreed:
   - Finance and Investment
   - Civil Aviation
   - Visas and Consular Services
   - Innovation, Trade and Economic Relations
   - Healthcare

- Science, Technology and Peaceful Uses of Outer Space
- Tourism, Culture and Sport
- Energy
- Environment
- Education
- Maritime Arrangements
- Telecommunications and Post
- Agriculture and Food Security
- Water
- Legal Cooperation

Any such agreements concluded before the entry into force of this Treaty shall enter into effect with the entry into force of this Treaty unless otherwise stipulated therein. Agreed principles for cooperation in specific spheres are annexed to this Treaty and form an integral part thereof.

6. **Mutual Understanding and Co-existence**: The Parties undertake to foster mutual understanding, respect, co-existence and a culture of peace between their societies in the spirit of their common ancestor, Abraham, and the new era of peace and friendly relations ushered in by this Treaty, including by cultivating people-to-people programs, interfaith dialogue and cultural, academic, youth, scientific, and other exchanges between their peoples. They shall conclude and implement the necessary visa and consular services agreements and arrangements so as to facilitate efficient and secure travel for their respective nationals to the territory of each other. The Parties shall work together to counter extremism, which promotes hatred and division, and terrorism and its justifications, including by preventing radicalization and recruitment and by combating incitement and

discrimination. They shall work towards establishing a High-Level Joint Forum for Peace and Co-Existence dedicated to advancing these goals.

7. **Strategic Agenda for the Middle East**: Further to the Abraham Accords, the Parties stand ready to join with the United States to develop and launch a "Strategic Agenda for the Middle East" in order to expand regional diplomatic, trade, stability and other cooperation. They are committed to work together, and with the United States and others, as appropriate, in order to advance the cause of peace, stability and prosperity in the relations between them and for the Middle East as a whole, including by seeking to advance regional security and stability; pursue regional economic opportunities; promote a culture of peace across the region; and consider joint aid and development programs.

8. **Other Rights and Obligations**: This Treaty does not affect and shall not be interpreted as affecting, in any way, the rights and obligations of the Parties under the Charter of the United Nations. The Parties shall take all necessary measures for the application in their bilateral relations of the provisions of the multilateral conventions of which they are both parties, including the submission of appropriate notification to the depositaries of such conventions.

9. **Respect for Obligations**: The Parties undertake to fulfill in good faith their obligations under this Treaty, without regard to action or inaction of any other party and independently of any instrument inconsistent with this Treaty. For the purposes of this paragraph each Party represents to the other that in its opinion and interpretation there is no inconsistency between their existing treaty

obligations and this Treaty. The Parties undertake not to enter into any obligation in conflict with this Treaty. Subject to Article 103 of the Charter of the United Nations, in the event of a conflict between the obligations of the Parties under the present Treaty and any of their other obligations, the obligations under this Treaty shall be binding and implemented. The Parties further undertake to adopt any legislation or other internal legal procedure necessary in order to implement this Treaty, and to repeal any national legislation or official publications inconsistent with this Treaty.

10. **Ratification and Entry into Force**: This Treaty shall be ratified by both Parties as soon as practicable in conformity with their respective national procedures and will enter into force following the exchange of instruments of ratification.

11. **Settlement of Disputes**: Disputes arising out of the application or interpretation of this Treaty shall be resolved by negotiation. Any such dispute which cannot be settled by negotiation may be referred to conciliation or arbitration subject to the agreement of the Parties.

12. **Registration**: This Treaty shall be transmitted to the Secretary-General of the United Nations for registration in accordance with the provisions of Article 102 of the Charter of the United Nations.

Done at Washington, DC, this day Elul 26th, 5780, Muharram 27th, 1442, which corresponds to 15 September 2020, in the Hebrew, Arabic and English languages, all texts being equally authentic. In case of divergence of interpretation, the English text shall prevail.

For the State of Israel:
H.E. Benjamin Netanyahu, Prime Minister

For the United Arab Emirates:
H. H. Abdullah bin Zayed Al Nahyan, Minister of
  Foreign Affairs and International Cooperation

Witnessed by:
H.E. Donald J. Trump, President of the United States
  of America

ANNEX

Pursuant to Article 5 of the Treaty of Peace, Diplomatic Relations and Full Normalization between the United Arab Emirates and the State of Israel, the Parties shall conclude bilateral agreements in spheres of mutual interest, in furtherance of which they have agreed to the following provisions. Such provisions are annexed to the Treaty and form an integral part thereof.

FINANCE AND INVESTMENT

Further to the Agreed Protocol signed between the Parties on September 1, 2020, in Abu Dhabi, the Parties shall cooperate to expeditiously deepen and broaden bilateral investment relations, and give high priority to concluding agreements in the sphere of finance and investment, recognizing the key role of these agreements in the economic development of the Parties and the Middle East as a whole. The Parties reaffirm their commitment to protecting investors, consumers, market integrity and financial stability, as well as maintaining all applicable regulatory standards. Recognizing also their shared goal to advance regional economic development and the flow of goods and services, the Parties shall endeavor to promote collaborations on strategic regional infrastructure projects and shall explore the establishment of a multilateral working group for the "Tracks for Regional Peace" project.

CIVIL AVIATION

The Parties acknowledge the importance of ensuring regular direct flights between Israel and the United Arab Emirates, for passengers and cargo, as an essential means for developing and promoting their relations. They recognize as applicable to each other the rights, privileges and obligations provided for by the multilateral aviation agreements to which they are both a party, their annexes and any amendments thereof applicable to both Parties, particularly the 1944 Convention on International Civil Aviation, opened for signature at Chicago on the seventh day of December 1944, and the 1944 International Air Services Transit Agreement. Accordingly, the Parties shall as soon as practicable conclude all the necessary agreements and arrangements governing civil aviation, and consequently work towards establishing an international air corridor between their two States in accordance with international law. They shall also reach and implement the necessary agreements and arrangements with respect to visas and consular services to facilitate travel for the citizens of both States.

TOURISM

The Parties affirm their mutual desire to promote tourism cooperation between them as a key component of economic development and of developing closer people-to-people and cultural ties. To this end, the Parties shall facilitate the exchange of information through advertisement spots, published and audiovisual promotional materials, and participation in tourist fairs. They shall also work together to promote joint tourism projects and packages between tourist operators so as to enhance tourism from third States. They shall work towards carrying out reciprocal study tours in order to increase knowledge in the development, management and marketing of heritage, cultural and rural tourism with a view to diversifying and deepening touristic links between them; and endeavor to utilize national marketing budgets to promote mutual tourism between the States.

INNOVATION, TRADE AND ECONOMIC RELATIONS

The Parties shall enhance and expand their cooperation in innovation, trade and economic relations, so that the dividends of peace are felt across their societies. Recognizing that the principle of the free and unimpeded flow of goods and services should guide their relations, as well as the potential for diversification of bilateral trade opportunities, the Parties shall cooperate in order to enable favorable conditions for trade, and the reduction of trade barriers.

SCIENCE, TECHNOLOGY AND PEACEFUL USES OF OUTER-SPACE

The Parties acknowledge the important role of science, technology and innovation in the growth of multiple key sectors and shall strengthen joint action and mutual cooperation in scientific and technological advancement. This shall include furthering scientific cooperation and exchange, including between scientists, research and academic institutions, pursuing the establishment of joint research and development centers, and exploring the possibility of joint funding of research and scientific projects in select fields of mutual interest.

The Parties further express their common interest in establishing and developing mutually beneficial cooperation in the field of exploration and use of outer space for peaceful purposes, in a manner consistent with each Party's respective applicable national laws and international obligations. Such cooperation may include implementation of joint programs, projects and activities in the fields of science, space exploration, space related technologies and education, exchange of experts, information and best practices, and the promotion of cooperation between their respective space industries.

ENVIRONMENT

The Parties acknowledge the importance of protecting, preserving and improving the environment, and shall promote environmental innovation for the sustainable development of the region and beyond. The Parties shall endeavor to cooperate to develop environmental protection strategies on priority issues, including on biodiversity conservation,

marine environment protection and climate change miti-
gation and adaptation, and on the possible establishment
of a center for developing pioneering solutions to climate
challenges in arid and semi-arid environments.

TELECOMMUNICATIONS AND POST

The Parties recognize the necessity of mutually beneficial
cooperation for the continued development of telecommunications, information technologies and postal services. They take note of the establishment between them
of direct communications services, including telephone
lines, and agree to promote, in accordance with relevant
international conventions and regulations, direct postal
exchange, submarine cables and e-commerce solutions,
as well as utilize available satellite systems, fiber opti-
cal communication, and broadcasting services. The Parties will strive to develop frameworks for innovation in
ICT, including advanced fixed and wireless communications, collaboration on 5G networks, smart cities, and
use of ICT solutions to foster innovation and the creation
of best services.

HEALTHCARE

The Parties welcome progress made in cooperation
between them regarding the treatment of, and the development of a vaccine for, the Covid-19 virus, as a sign of
the tremendous potential for cooperation between them
in the healthcare sphere. Recognizing the importance
of building ties in the fields of health and medicine, the
Parties shall cooperate, inter alia, on: medical education,

training and simulations, digital health and artificial intelligence innovation in the health sector, and emergency management and preparedness.

AGRICULTURE AND FOOD SECURITY

The Parties recognize the great importance of sustainable agricultural development, recognizing its vital role in addressing food security concerns, as well as in the preservation of the environment. They shall cooperate to harness and maximize existing technologies, actively facilitate new collaborations, and share and develop knowledge, technologies and innovative approaches in the field of arid agriculture, irrigation technologies, mariculture techniques in shallow sea water, sustainable nutritious fish feed production, and seed enhancement in hot and humid climates.

WATER

The Parties recognize the critical importance of sustainable water use and shall cooperate for their mutual benefit to address issues of water supply, water treatment and management, water security, efficiency, wastewater management and reuse, as well as water conservation and desalination.

ENERGY

The Parties take note of the strategic importance of the energy sector and in particular of their need to promote renewable energy, cooperation in the natural gas field, regional grids, alternative energy and energy security. They shall advance and develop mutual cooperation in energy projects, share best practices and discuss policies in energy forums that will help to promote and unlock the energy potential of the region, coordinating where appropriate with the International Renewable Energy Agency (IRENA), headquartered in Abu Dhabi.

MARITIME ARRANGEMENTS

Each Party shall recognize the right of vessels of the other Party to innocent passage through its territorial waters in accordance with international law. Each Party will grant normal access to its ports for vessels and cargoes of the other Party, as well as vessels and cargoes destined for or coming from the other Party. Such access shall be granted on the same terms as generally applicable to vessels and cargoes of other nations. The Parties shall conclude agreements and arrangements in maritime affairs, as may be required.

LEGAL COOPERATION

Recognizing the importance of a supporting legal framework for the movement of people and goods and for fostering a continuous business friendly environment between them, the Parties shall make best efforts to grant each other the widest measure of legal cooperation, including, inter alia, in respect of mutual legal assistance in civil and commercial matters, in accordance with their national laws and shall endeavor to conclude specific agreements and arrangements in this sphere.

ABRAHAM ACCORDS: DECLARATION OF PEACE, COOPERATION, AND CONSTRUCTIVE DIPLOMATIC AND FRIENDLY RELATIONS

Announced by the State of Israel and the Kingdom of Bahrain on 15 September 2020

His Majesty King Hamad bin Isa bin Salman al-Khalifa and Prime Minister Benjamin Netanyahu have agreed to open an era of friendship and cooperation in pursuit of a Middle East region that is stable, secure and prosperous for the benefit of all States and peoples in the region. In this spirit Prime Minister Netanyahu floral and Foreign Minister Mr. Abdullatif Al Zayani met in Washington today, at the invitation of President Donald J. Trump of the United States of America, to endorse the principles of the Abraham Accords and to commence a new chapter of peace. This diplomatic breakthrough was facilitated by the Abraham Accords initiative of President Donald J. Trump. It reflects the successful perseverance of the United States' efforts to promote peace and stability in the Middle East. The Kingdom of Bahrain and the State of Israel trust that this development will help lead to a future in which all peoples and all faiths can live together in the spirit of cooperation and enjoy peace and prosperity where states focus on shared interests and building a better future.

The parties discussed their shared commitment to advancing peace and security in the Middle East stressing the importance of embracing the vision of the Abraham Accords, widening the circle of peace; recognizing each State's right to sovereignty and to live in peace and security, and continuing the efforts to achieve a just, comprehensive, and enduring resolution of the Israeli-Palestinian conflict.

In their meeting, Prime Minister Benjamin Netanyahu and Foreign Minister Abdullatif Al Zayani agreed to establish full diplomatic relations, to promote lasting security, to eschew threats and the use of force, as well as advance coexistence and a culture of peace. In this spirit, they have today approved a series of steps initiating this new chapter in their relations. The Kingdom of Bahrain and the State of Israel have agreed to seek agreements in the coming weeks regarding investment, tourism, direct flights, security, telecommunications, technology, energy, health care, culture, the environment, and other areas of mutual benefit, as well as reaching agreement on the reciprocal opening of embassies.

The Kingdom of Bahrain and the State of Israel view this moment as a historic opportunity and recognize their responsibility to pursue a more secure and prosperous future for generations to come in their respective countries and in the region.

The two countries jointly express their profound thanks and appreciation to President Donald J. Trump for his untiring efforts and unique and pragmatic approach to further the cause of peace, justice and prosperity for all the peoples of the region. In recognition of this appreciation, the two countries have asked President Donald J. Trump to sign this document as a witness to their shared resolve and as the host of their historic meeting.

Prime Minister Benjamin Netanyahu
Foreign Minister Abdullatif Al Zayani
Witnessed by President Donald J. Trump

THE ABRAHAM ACCORDS DECLARATION:

We, the undersigned, recognize the importance of maintaining and strengthening peace in the Middle East and around the world based on mutual understanding and coexistence, as well as respect for human dignity and freedom, including religious freedom.

We encourage efforts to promote interfaith and intercultural dialogue to advance a culture of peace among the three Abrahamic religions and all humanity.

We believe that the best way to address challenges is through cooperation and dialogue and that developing friendly relations among States advances the interests of lasting peace in the Middle East and around the world.

We seek tolerance and respect for every person in order to make this world a place where all can enjoy a life of dignity and hope, no matter their race, faith or ethnicity.

We support science, art, medicine, and commerce to inspire humankind, maximize human potential and bring nations closer together.

We seek to end radicalization and conflict to provide all children a better future.

We pursue a vision of peace, security, and prosperity in the Middle East and around the world.

In this spirit, we warmly welcome and are encouraged by the progress already made in establishing diplomatic relations between Israel and its neighbors in the region under the principles of the Abraham Accords. We are encouraged by the ongoing efforts to consolidate and expand such friendly relations based on shared interests and a shared commitment to a better future.

For the Republic of Sudan:
Justice Minister Nasredeen Abdulbari

Witnessed
Treasury Secretary Steven Mnuchin

JOINT DECLARATION

The Kingdom of Morocco, The United States of America and the State of Israel,

Referring to the telephone conversation held between His Majesty King Mohammed VI and His Excellency President Donald Trump, on 10 December 2020, and to the historic statements issued on the same day by them, and by His Excellency Prime Minister Benjamin Netanyahu of the State of Israel, announcing the opening of a new era in the relations between the Kingdom of Morocco and the State of Israel;

Welcoming the opportunity created through the extraordinary efforts and leadership of the United States;

Highlighting the proclamation by the United States of America on "Recognizing the Sovereignty of the Kingdom of Morocco over the Western Sahara," according to which:

- "The United States recognizes Moroccan sovereignty over the entire Western Sahara territory and reaffirms its support for Morocco's serious, credible, and realistic autonomy proposal as the only basis for a just and lasting solution to the dispute over the Western Sahara territory."

- "To facilitate progress toward this aim, the United States will encourage economic and social development with Morocco, including in the Western Sahara territory, and to that end will open a consulate in the Western Sahara territory, in Dakhla, to promote economic and business opportunities for the region."

Recalling the exchanged views, during the same conversation between His Majesty King Mohammed VI and His Excellency Donald Trump, on the current situation in the Middle East region in which His Majesty the King reiterated the coherent, constant and unchanged position of the Kingdom of Morocco on the Palestinian question, as well as the position expressed on the importance of preserving the special status of the sacred city of Jerusalem for the three monotheistic religions in His Majesty the King's capacity as Chairman of the Al-Quds Committee;

Recognizing the historic role that Morocco has always played in bringing the people of the region closer together and promoting peace and stability in the Middle East, and given the special ties that His Majesty maintains with the Moroccan Jewish community living in Morocco and throughout the world including in Israel;

Mindful that the establishment of full diplomatic, peaceful and friendly relations is in the common interest of both countries and will advance the cause of peace in the region, improve regional security, and unlock new opportunities for the whole region;

Recalling the conversation between His Majesty King Mohammed VI and His Excellency Donald Trump, His Majesty the King affirmed that the Kingdom of Morocco and the State of Israel intend to:

- Grant authorizations for direct flights between Morocco and Israel, including by Israeli and Moroccan airline companies, as well as grant rights of overflight; Immediately resume full official contacts between Israeli and Moroccan counterparts and establish full diplomatic, peaceful and friendly relations;
- Promote a dynamic and innovative economic bilateral cooperation;
- Pursue cooperation on trade; finance and investment; innovation and technology; civil aviation; visas and consular services; tourism; water, agriculture, and food security; development; energy and telecommunications; and other sectors as may be agreed;
- Reopen the liaison offices in Rabat and Tel Aviv.

Based on the above, the Kingdom of Morocco, the United States of America and the State of Israel agree to:

1. Commit to fully respect the elements contained in the present Declaration, promote it and defend it;
2. Decide that each party will fully implement its commitments and identify further actions, before the end of January;
3. Act accordingly at the bilateral, regional and multilateral levels.

Done at Rabat, 22 December 2020

For the Kingdom of Morocco
Mr. Saad Dine El Otmani
Chief of Government

For the United States of America
Mr. Jarred Kushner
Senior Advisor to the President

For the State of Israel
Mr. Meir Ben-Shabbat
National Security Advisor and of the National Security
   Council

Mr. Alon Ushpiz
Director General Ministry of Foreign Affairs

About the Author

DAVID FRIEDMAN served as the U.S. ambassador to Israel from 2017 to 2021. Under his leadership, the United States made unprecedented and historic diplomatic advances, including moving its embassy to Jerusalem and recognizing Israel's sovereignty over the Golan Heights. Ambassador Friedman was also one of the architects of the Abraham Accords. For his efforts, he was nominated for a Nobel Peace Prize and granted the National Security Medal.

On numerous occasions, the *Jerusalem Post* has named Ambassador Friedman one of the fifty most influential Jews in the world—he rose to number two in 2019 and number one in 2020. In 2021, the *New York Times* described him "as one of America's most influential envoys" and as someone "who drove the radical overhaul of White House policy toward the Israeli-Palestinian conflict."

Ambassador Friedman is the bestselling author of *Sledgehammer: How Breaking with the Past Brought Peace to the Middle East* and the executive producer and co-star, with former Secretary of State Mike Pompeo, of *Route 60: The Biblical Highway*, a film about Judea and Samaria. In 2021, he opened the Friedman Center for Peace through

Strength, which has recently launched a project that bears the name of this book: One Jewish State.

He lives with his wife, Tammy, in Jerusalem and Florida and is a proud father and grandfather.

To learn more about the One Jewish State movement and get involved, go to OneJewishState.net.